BISHOP EAST OF THE ROCKIES

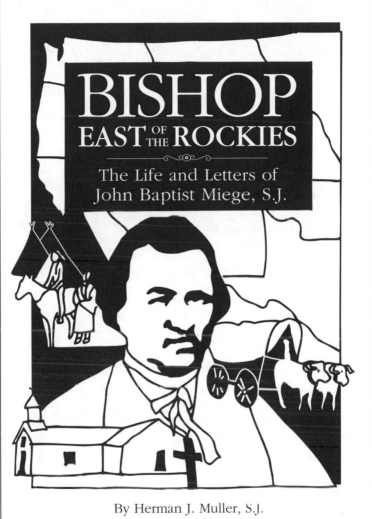

BISHOP
EAST OF THE ROCKIES

The Life and Letters of
John Baptist Miege, S.J.

By Herman J. Muller, S.J.
Foreword by
James J. Hennesey, S.J.

A Campion Book
Loyola University Press
Chicago

Loyola University Press
3441 North Ashland Avenue
Chicago, Illinois 60657

Cover and interior design by Nancy Gruenke.
Cover art by Robert Masheris.

Library of Congress Cataloging-in-Publication Data
Muller, Herman J. (Herman Joseph), 1909-
    Bishop east of the Rockies: the life and letters of John Baptist
Miege, S.J./by Herman Muller, S.J.
        p.   cm.
    Includes bibliographical references and index.
    ISBN 0-8294-0780-4
    1. Miege, John Baptist, 1815-1884. 2. Catholic Church—
United States—Bishops—Biography. 3. Jesuits—United States
Biography.
    I. Title.
    BX4705.M55234M85   1994
    282'.092—dc20
    (B)   93-42171
                                                                           CIP

CONTENTS

ILLUSTRATIONS

FOREWORD

It is good to have Bishop John Baptist Miege, S. J., rescued from the mists of midnineteenth century history. I first came to know of him from his tombstone in the Woodstock College cemetery in Maryland. Jesuits have pretty uniform tombstones. They give the man's name and the dates of his birth, entrance into the Society, and death. That brief catalog is topped by the IHS symbol of the order, followed by the final prayer: "R.I.P., May he rest in peace."

Father Miege's grave marker stood out. For one thing, it was larger than the rest. This was probably because it had to accommodate his episcopal titles. He was ordained on March 25, 1851, as titular bishop of Messene and served from that date until 1874 as vicar apostolic of the Indian Territory, east of the Rocky Mountains. But that was not all.

A refugee from the European revolutions of 1848, Miege had come to the Jesuits' Missouri vice-province to share in its work among Native Americans. His tenure as vicar apostolic, based in Leavenworth, Kansas, saw the transformation of the region into a normally functioning diocese, but not before Miege had many a frontier adventure in a jurisdiction that reached as far west as Colorado. He had accepted the miter reluctantly and believed that, as a Jesuit, he should set it down once the vicariate ceased to be of a primarily missionary nature.

But first he had to live through the travails of "bleeding Kansas" and the Civil War, which severely divided his diocesans. He participated in the Vatican Council of 1869–70, where he was one of a minority among the bishops of the United States who vigorously supported the definition of papal infallibility. Most of the rest thought the step inopportune, while another minority led by his own metropolitan, Archbishop Kenrick, were outright opponents. This did not faze Miege, who was, in his own unassuming way, a thoroughgoing ultramontane.

One last hurdle had to be jumped before he could resume the ordinary life of a Jesuit priest, however. He had to bring the large diocesan debt under control, which he did, in part, by a "begging" tour in South America. His resignation as vicar apostolic was accepted on November 18, 1874, and he retired first to St. Louis University and then to the new Woodstock College as spiritual director. But there was still one last administrative task asked of him and that was to be appointed founding rector and president of the new Jesuit college in Detroit, a position he held successfully for three years before returning to his quiet duties at Woodstock.

Father Muller has told Miege's story as it happened, without embroidery. We get a fine sense of the kind of person the bishop was, of the difficult problems he faced, and how he handled them. This is no plaster saint, but a real-life, flesh-and-blood human being, devoted to the Church, to the Society of Jesus within the Church, and to the people of his vast missionary diocese. It is good to have this record of his life and times, well told by a veteran historian.

James J. Hennesey, S. J.
Canisius Jesuit Community
Buffalo, New York

INTRODUCTION

This biography tells the story of the Savoy-born Jesuit John Baptist Miege, who came to the United States in 1848 as a missionary to the Native Americans of the Great Plains. John Baptist received his early education in French-speaking Savoy, at the time a part of the kingdom of Sardinia. In 1836, at the age of twenty-one, he entered the Society of Jesus at Milan. John Baptist was ordained to the priesthood in Rome in 1847 and completed his studies the following year. Meanwhile he had asked to be sent to the American missions. His request was granted. Arriving in the States, he began his work in the area around St. Louis, Missouri, dividing his time working in the nearby Indian settlement, at Florissant, Missouri, where there was a house of studies for young Jesuits, and as an instructor at St. Louis University. It was while Miege was at the university that he was appointed vicar apostolic (bishop) of the Indian Territory.

In 1851 the Indian Territory, some 500,000 square miles, comprised roughly the area from the Rocky Mountains to Missouri and from the Canadian border to New Mexico. Bishop Miege was a true pioneer in this vast territory. His travels with two mules hitched to an old St. Louis milk wagon, his dealings with the Native Americans, his presence at the opening of the Territory by the Kansas-Nebraska Act of 1854, his personal witness to the gold strikes at Pike's Peak, his presence in Lawrence, Kansas, when Quantrill was raiding the town, all make for a fascinating study. Bishop Miege retired as bishop of Leavenworth, Kansas, in 1874. After a few years at Woodstock College, Maryland, he was called on, in 1877, to become the first president of the Detroit College, later the University of Detroit. He filled that position with distinction to 1881, when he returned to Woodstock College to serve as counselor to the students there. He died a few years later on July 21, 1884.

Recalling Miege's description of the Indians and their customs, M. Whitcomb Hess wrote in the *Contemporary Review*:

Such pictures help us reconstruct something of mid-nineteenth century life in America. Whether the writer describes his long trip to the Colorado goldfields in 1860 . . . or his visit to Lawrence, Kansas, during Quantrill's raid (1863) . . . or his day-by-day accounts of life among the Indians, the Bishop wrote with consistent compassion and understanding of his fellowmen. Certainly he championed the Indians and did all in his power to mitigate where he could not prevent American persecution of this country's first inhabitants. He was . . . himself an American.

Bishop Miege provides an excellent example of an early Midwestern pioneer clergyman. His story adds to our sense of roots and to the history of Kansas, Nebraska, eastern Colorado, and, in his later years, Detroit. Finally, it is indeed a shame that, with the possible exception of Kansas, this truly great pioneer bishop has remained so comparatively unknown. We hope that our humble effort may lead to further research in his regard in the near future. Perhaps another Willa Cather will come along and do justice to his story in the same way that she did for his dear friend Bishop J. B. Lamy of New Mexico in her *Death Comes for the Archbishop.*

The archives cited throughout the biography are indicated by the following abbreviations:

(LUA) Loyola University (Chicago) Archives.

(MPA) Missouri Province Archives.

(SLA) St. Louis Province of the Society of Jesus Archives.

(UDA) University of Detroit Archives.

In addition, the Kansas City, Kansas, Diocesan Archives; Benedictine Abbey Archives at Atchison, Kansas; the Saint Mary's College Archives at Leavenworth, Kansas; and the State Archives at Topeka, Kansas, have been consulted with profit. The main library in Leavenworth has the early Leavenworth newspapers on microfilm.

Most of the Miege letters consulted throughout the biography are found in Joseph Garin's *Notices Biographiques sur Mgr. J.-B. Miége Premier Vicaire Apostolique du Kansas.* Copies of this work are very scarce. One copy is located in the Bibliothèque nationale in Paris. The translation used throughout is that of the author. Other sources are indicated in the notes.

I am most grateful to the Reverend Clayton Schario, S.J., who read and helped me with the manuscript and who somehow managed to keep the kinks out of my computer. Special thanks are due to the Detroit Province of the Society of Jesus and to Enterprise Rent-A-Car for grants that made my research possible. In addition, I would like to thank the archivists and librarians whose cooperation was of great help, particularly Brother Michael Grace, S.J., of Loyola University (Chicago), and Father William Barnaby Faherty, S.J., of St. Louis. I must also mention the assistance and constant encouragement of friends in Kansas, especially the Reverend William McEvoy and William Brady, J. H. Johnston III, and John Biringer Miller, Jr. A final word of acknowledgment is due to the Reverend Joseph Downey, S.J., and his staff at Loyola University Press for helping bring this biography to its completion.

CHRONOLOGY

1815 September 18: John Baptist Miege is born in La Forêt, Chevron, Savoy, the twelfth of fourteen children.

1828 Miege enters College of Moûtiers in Savoy.

1834 Miege completes his classical studies.

1836 October 23: Miege enters the Society of Jesus in Milan.

1838 October 15: Miege takes his first vows of poverty, chastity, and obedience.

1842 Miege serves as chief disciplinarian at a Jesuit boarding school in Milan.

1844 The Society sends Miege to the Roman College for theological study.

1847 September 12: Miege is ordained to the priesthood in Rome.

1848 Father General John Roothaan grants Miege permission to serve the missions in North America.
June 1: Miege sails for America on the vessel *Providence*.

1849 The Seventh Provincial Council of Baltimore petitions Pope Pius IX to erect a vicariate in the Indian Territory.

1850 July 23: Pope Pius IX appoints Miege vicar apostolic of the 500,000-square mile Indian Territory.

1851 March 25: Miege is consecrated bishop in Saint Francis Xavier Church, St. Louis, Missouri. He takes up residence among the Potawatomie Indians at Saint Mary's Mission, Kansas.

1853   March: Miege is elected to represent the Missouri province at the Twenty-second General Congregation of the Society of Jesus in Rome.

April: Miege sets out for Europe to raise funds for his American missions; he visits with Pope Pius IX.

1855   August 9: Miege leaves Saint Mary's Mission to relocate to Leavenworth, Kansas. A few days later, he formally establishes the Cathedral Parish of the Immaculate Conception.

1857   February 17: At Miege's behest, Pope Pius IX creates the Vicariate of Nebraska.

1858   November: Miege persuades the Sisters of Charity to establish a community in Leavenworth. Within several months, they open Saint Mary's Academy for Young Ladies. Five years later they would also establish Saint John's, the first civilian hospital in Kansas.

1860   May 26: Miege arrives in Denver during the Colorado gold rush and spends some time administering to the spiritual needs of the miners.

1863   August 21: William Quantrill and his band of raiders destroy the town of Lawrence, Kansas. Miege consoles the frightened townspeople.

1864   September 18: Cornerstone of the Cathedral of the Immaculate Conception placed, Leavenworth, Kansas.

1868   December 8: Dedication of Cathedral of the Immaculate Conception, Leavenworth, Kansas.

1869   December 8: Vatican Council opens with Bishop Miege in attendance.

1871   June: Bishop Louis Mary Fink, O.S.B., is appointed Miege's coadjutor.

October 12: Miege departs for South America on a fund-raising trip to reduce the cathedral debt.

1874 May 25: Miege returns to Leavenworth.

November 18: Pius IX accepts John Baptist's request for resignation. Miege retires as bishop of Leavenworth, Kansas.

1875 Miege becomes spiritual director of the Jesuits at Woodstock College, Maryland.

1877 Miege becomes the first president of Detroit College (later the University of Detroit).

1881 Miege returns to Woodstock College, Maryland, to serve as counselor; signs his last will and testament.

1884 July 21: John Baptist Miege dies, Woodstock, Maryland.

1

EARLY YEARS

The year 1848 marked a turning point for many European Jesuits. Multiple revolutions threw Europe into turmoil. Nationalism and liberalism, twin legacies of the French Revolution that had been temporarily held in check by the Congress of Vienna, were again running rampant. In the German states, university students formed secret societies to fight for unification and reform. In Russia, the Decembrists clamored for liberal reforms after the death of Alexander I. In Spain, mutiny and revolt were ruthlessly suppressed by Ferdinand VII. Meanwhile, Milan Obrenović was leading his Serbs to freedom, and Alexandros Ypsilantis made a bid to free the Greeks. In 1830 the Poles tried to free themselves from Russian control, and Belgium became independent of Holland. In Italy, led by such ardent spirits as Giuseppe Garibaldi, Giuseppe Mazzini, and Camillo Cavour, liberals insisted that the Austrians be driven out of the north and the pope out of the Papal States. Rome alone could be the capital of a unified Italy.

On February 10, 1848, the government of Savoy ordered the Jesuits to leave their college in Chambéry within twenty-four hours. On the night of February 28 screams of "death to the Jesuits" were heard outside the College of Genoa. A few days later, when a group of Jesuits landed in the Gulf of La

Right Reverend John Baptist Miege, S. J. (1815–84).
Courtesy Kansas State Historical Society, Topeka,
Kansas.

Spezia on their way into exile, they were greeted with similar
cries and were slung with mud and pelted with stones.

Why all this hatred of the Jesuits? To begin with, they were
known as champions of legitimate authority. When they
returned to France after the restoration of the French monar-
chy, liberals associated them, rightly or wrongly, with abso-
lutism, the divine right of kings, and the *ancien regime* in
general. As advocates of the Holy See they were regarded as
natural enemies of liberals and nationals alike. There could be
no question where the Jesuits stood in Italy regarding the con-
fiscation of the Papal States.

The houses of the Society of Jesus in Rome, as elsewhere,
were closed. Among the Jesuits who betook themselves to the

port of Rome at Civitavecchia to sail to Marseilles was the hero of our story, John Baptist Miege.[1] But there was a difference. Arriving at the port ahead of his brethren, he so well disguised himself as completely to outwit the officers of the vessel on which he was to sail. Miege was a tall, stately, handsome man; a fine beard made him all the more impressive. Everybody on board took him for an Italian nobleman. John Baptist was not averse to taking advantage of the situation. "Assuming the role of protector of the exiles, his address was so bold, his rebukes and his orders so peremptory" that nobody dared contradict him. The result was that his brethren fared well on their trip to Marseilles.[2]

John Baptist Miege, the twelfth of fourteen children of Balthazard and Josephte Miege, was born on September 18, 1815, at La Forêt, a village in the parish of Chevron, diocese of Moûtiers, Savoy, a French-speaking area southwest of Switzerland.

The year 1815 was most important in European affairs. In June, three months before the birth of John Baptist, the final act of the Congress of Vienna was signed. Though the traditional principles of the Congress—legitimacy, balance of power, and compensation—were not always adhered to, and though the conservatism of the Congress was soon to end in disaster, the fact remains that the alliance of the Great Powers did manage to maintain the peace. There were no major wars during John Baptist's childhood.

The Miege family originated in Pallud in Savoy and then, from the seventeenth century onward, dwelt in Frontenex, a parish of Cléry. The Mieges were not of the nobility, nor were they particularly wealthy. Rather they were good, simple, honorable farmers who even before moving to La Forêt in 1808 had given more than their share of prominent persons to the service of church and state.[3] In 1808 Balthazard Miege inherited a share of the property that his uncle, the Reverend Jean-Louis Miege, canon of Tarentaise, owned in the village of La Forêt. With this improvement in their financial condition the Mieges moved to La Forêt some seven years before the birth of John Baptist. Not much is known about John Baptist's early childhood. After Miege's death in 1884, Father Paul Ponziglione, S.J., prevailed upon the Very Reverend James Defouri, vicar general of Santa Fe, New Mexico, to write down his recollections. Defouri had known Miege as a boy and had worked with him in Leavenworth, Kansas, for several years.[4]

Except for an error in the number of children in the Miege family—Defouri said five rather than fourteen—we may value Defouri's document as more than the ramblings of an old friend.[5] After referring to John Baptist's "truly Christian" parents, Defouri states: "Early in life he learned at his pious mother's knees to lisp the tender names of Jesus and Mary. They had also a beautiful family chapel where frequently the young boy heard mass with raptures of piety, and afterwards served it with angelic fervor, which drew tears from the eyes of the simple people present."[6] John Baptist may have been this pious as a small boy, but we suspect, judging from his early school years, that given the opportunity he would not have been above blasting off a cannon in the middle of the night as Saint Aloysius Gonzaga once did. He had a bit of the prankster in his makeup. We are told that, when he became an American bishop, his former school companions back home thought it a "tremendous joke" that "such a little rascal" should be so honored.

Like most of the children in the village, John Baptist was a shepherd until he was ready for his secondary education. One of his brothers, Urban-Louis, thirteen years his senior, made use of his vacation periods from college to give his little brother a basic training in reading and writing. When Urban, once ordained, became professor of grammar at the College of Conflans in Savoy in 1826, he took his young brother with him. John Baptist remained at Conflans for two years. In 1828 Urban was named professor of grammar and belles lettres at the college and minor seminary of Moûtiers in Savoy. John Baptist followed him there. He was fortunate indeed in having so wise a sibling to watch over him, to counsel him, and to serve as a father figure.[7] In return, John Baptist manifested the greatest love and affection for his older brother.

It soon developed that the young man was not a great scholar. Apparently he found recreation more to his liking than serious study. He was ever full of good humor, and to the end of his life he remained a consummate tease. Meanwhile, Urban handled him kindly, yet firmly, curbing his early pranks with no little energy.[8] Father A. Usannaz, S.J., one of John Baptist's fellow novices in the Society of Jesus, spoke of Urban as "a severe disciplinarian who did not deal indulgently with his own brother and punished him severely."[9] In those days teachers did not "spare the rod." Still, judging from his character—and the final results—the teacher, in this case, was not overly severe. Miege's biographer, Joseph Garin, has nothing but praise for this good man who had so profound an influence on the future bishop. Since the vast majority of John Baptist's letters from America were addressed to his brother, it will not be out of order to include at least a summary of Garin's eulogy of Urban here.[10]

Urban-Louis Miege taught for thirty-one years at the College of Moûtiers. Throughout this period he was much devoted to study. He was a man of strict observance of rules and of kindness toward his colleagues as well as his students. Above all he was an exemplary priest as shown by his piety and his spirit of personal abnegation. In addition to his teaching assignments, he performed, at various times, the sensitive roles of prefect of discipline for the college, spiritual director, and prefect of studies. He had a talent for music and delighted in giving special lessons to some of his students. Moreover, on Thursdays and Sundays during the school year, he gave lessons in chant to the community.

After thirty-six years, he was finally permitted to enjoy a well-merited rest. This by no means meant complete inactivity. Named honorary canon of the Cathedral by the bishop of Tarentaise, he spent the remaining fifteen years of his life in La Forêt helping his family and the parish of Chevron. He taught Latin to a large number of young men, some of whom became priests and stayed in the area; others became priests and served at foreign missions. Meanwhile he continued giving music lessons to the young men and women "whose harmonious chants brought great splendor to the stately feasts so greatly enjoyed by the parishioners and so pleasing to the zealous Curé of Chevron. . . ." In 1870, the venerable Canon Miege had, for the last time, the pleasure of seeing his much beloved brother when the latter returned from attending Vatican I. Urban-Louis Miege died December 12, 1874. Defouri, who also had high praise for the good canon, remarked that he received a letter from the bishop at the time, which stated simply: "My brother Urban is dead, please pray for him."[11]

Years earlier, John Baptist had been only nineteen years old when he completed his classical studies. One morning, about to return to La Forêt for the summer, he approached his brother to ask for his approval to join the army. Urban was painfully surprised to hear of his decision to become a soldier, but, fully aware of the turmoil that prevailed in early nineteenth-century Europe, he gave his consent. Urban saw the country "convulsed by wars and rumors of wars." It was not surprising that the military spirit should have penetrated the quiet halls of the college. Defouri states that the usual exercises of the boys when out-of-doors was to march, to drill, to play at being soldiers. The talented John Baptist caught the fever.[12] In giving his consent Urban imposed one condition; namely, that the young man first finish his course of philosophy. John Baptist readily consented. Two years later he again appeared before his brother. "Well, John Baptist?" asked Urban. "Brother, with your consent I would like to enter the Society of Jesus." "What about the army?" asked his brother. "Oh well, that is entering the army," replied the young philosopher.[13] Thereupon Urban gave his immediate consent and two weeks later, on October 23, 1836, John Baptist was admitted to the Society of Jesus in Milan.

2

THE YOUNG JESUIT

One wonders what caused this sudden change of heart in John Baptist. He never told us. Joseph Garin, though, offers one theory: "As he advanced in his classes," Garin wrote, "the young John Baptist, endowed with good common sense and a great strength of will, had the foresight to see that greater discipline could fortify him against a sort of natural listlessness. This happy thought incited him to enter the Society of Jesus after having completed his studies at the College of Moûtiers with somewhat mediocre success. . . ."[1] If we add to this John Baptist's basic goodness and the grace of God—who called him, like Paul, to be an apostle—we may be closer to the truth.

After a period of "first probation," a sort of spiritual initiation, John Baptist was admitted as a Jesuit novice in Milan. His spiritual director during these early years was Father Francis Pellico, later Italian assistant to the Father General John Roothaan. The young novice worked hard to master the virtues of his calling. His fellows were soon to witness in him a deep sense of charity, humility, and self-discipline, together with a fervent love of and devotion to his institute—virtues that were to remain with him throughout his life.[2] Years later, one of his fellow novices mentioned how, during a severe bout of sickness in 1837, he had occasion to admire "his

[Miege's] charity, his humility and his readiness to fulfill the lowest services devolving on infirmarians towards the sick, and his fidelity to religious observances."[3]

Brother Miege took his first vows of poverty, chastity, and obedience on October 15, 1838. There followed two years of juniorate, which he devoted in large part to the study of classical literature and, possibly, to a renewal of his philosophy. Since he had done his philosophical studies at Moûtiers, he did not follow his classical studies with a course in philosophy as was the custom of the Society at the time. Instead he began his term as a teaching scholastic, first at Aosta in northwestern Italy, then shortly thereafter at the famed Jesuit school at Chambéry, and, finally, in 1842, back at Milan.[4]

We are told that, while at Chambéry, his jovial and genial disposition and the fullness with which he sympathized with the students endeared him to them and rendered them "as pliable as wax in his hands."[5] Judging from a letter he wrote to his brother in May 1841, he must have been very much occupied with his new duties: "Don't be surprised if you have not received a letter from me recently. I am extremely busy; exams are approaching, time is short, and taking everything into consideration, I have the necessary means to satisfy my obligations and nothing more. For three months I have wanted to pay you back but have not managed to do so."[6] He also begged that God's will be done; he was willing to do whatever was asked of him with the greatest pleasure.

Toward the end of the same year, he wrote to his mother: "When I was at Moûtiers I recall receiving your gifts on the first day of the New Year; you are aware in what they usually consisted. I am writing to you today to wish you a Happy New Year and to ask you for some New Year gifts, not like the former ones, but for a few prayers for my intention, which you will say to our good Mother the Blessed Virgin, and to the good, little newly born infant Jesus." In the same letter John Baptist asked for a little Ave Maria from all the other members of the family, for himself, and for his dear deceased father. "That the will of the good God be done; but if he should wish it of me I shall most gladly go to him."[7] These few citations give us an idea of how detached from material goods the young Jesuit had become and how ready he was to follow the calling of Providence through the voice of his superiors.

In 1842, Brother Miege was sent to Milan where the Society operated a large boarding school. There he served as chief disciplinarian, a position for which he seems to have had a special aptitude. His tall, dignified appearance, modified by his manifest kindliness, inspired love as well as respect in his charges. He was so great a lover of regularity that his brothers in Christ were wont to refer jokingly to him as the *gendarme* of the college. No doubt John Baptist, recalling his own escapades as a youngster, was able to keep more than a step ahead of the boys at Milan.

Evidently his Jesuit superiors saw much promise in Brother Miege, since they decided in 1844 to send him to the celebrated Roman College for his theological studies. He did not disappoint them. He was particularly fortunate in his teachers at Rome. Among them were Father Francis Xavier Patrizi, the great authority in biblical studies, and Father Anthony Ballerini, the eminent moralist. Then there was the erudite Giovanni Perrone, conspicuous in the discussions that ended in the dogmatic definition of the Immaculate Conception and whose nine-volume *Praelectiones Theologiae* was published in thirty-four editions. Another teacher was the "brilliant but unfortunate" Carlo Passaglia, of whom writer Hugo Von Hurter once referred to as "an illustrious professor of dogma who was carried away by politics, left the Society, assailed the Temporal Power, and by his sad defection cast a stain on his former glory."[8]

Brother Miege did exceptionally well in his studies at the Roman College, especially in moral theology where his practical mind stood him in good stead. *The Catalogue for the Roman Province of the Society,* a Jesuit publication, informs us that during John Baptist's second and third years in Rome he devoted some of his spare time to teaching catechism to the inmates of a new government prison. In his final year he heard confessions at the same prison.[9] Brother Miege did not let his success change his personality in the least. One of his fellow students was later to remark: "During these first years of hard study Father Miege was the same as before, the jovial and good friend of all, the life of recreation even in the darkest days and circumstances."[10]

The days were indeed dark, particularly toward the end of Miege's stay in Rome. In early September 1847, he wrote to his brother Urban: "People are quite busy reviving the old hats of Voltaire and company against the Jesuits; they wear them in an Italian fashion and thus hooded cause them to travel to every nook and corner of Italy . . . . They even forward the newspapers that treat us so honorably to galley slaves! They reproach us with impeding progress, of suffocating the young folks committed to us under a heap of Latin and Greek rubbish; of favoring the cause of the Austrians against the freedom of Italy, etc. . . . . You would laugh on seeing our faces and witnessing the special greetings that we give their prejudices. Oh! how delightful if only good old Cicero could take part in these comedies!"[11] He added that words alone were not the only weapons used by these courageous enemies. He tells us how two of the Fathers traveling recently through Tuscany were pelted with stones to the cries of "Down with the Jesuits! Death to the Jesuits!" He continues: "After so dangerous a battle the assailants returned to their homes, to enjoy peacefully the sweetness of a triumph that Father De Smet's natives would have scorned. It would seem that, to the present, *progress* [claimed by the Liberals] cannot be seen as being exceptionally high, since the Blackfeet and Flatheads are infinitely superior in good manners and in cordiality, according to the most recent letters come from the forests of North America."[12]

Due to the unsettled conditions in Rome and elsewhere, Jesuit superiors decided to have their aspirants to the priesthood ordained somewhat earlier than usual. John Baptist Miege was ordained to the subdiaconate on September 5, 1847, and to the diaconate on the September 8. His ordination to the priesthood took place on September 12, 1847, shortly before his thirty-second birthday. He was ordained by Cardinal Canali in the latter's own private chapel.[13] Father Miege had the honor of saying his first mass in Saint Ignatius's living quarters in the Gesù, Rome, where Ignatius died. Saint Francis Borgia later lived there; Saint Charles Borromeo had said Mass there, and Saint Francis de Sales had visited the apartments. Father Miege said his second Mass in the room where Saint Aloysius Gonzaga had lived as a theologian.[14]

John Baptist said his third Mass at a lovely villa about twelve miles from Rome. It was there that he enjoyed a two-week vacation with some of his fellow students from the

Roman College. He then returned to the city for his last year of theological studies. His stated plan, as expressed in a letter to his brother, was to ready himself for his two-hour final examination in theology to take place in May 1848. He would then do his tertianship—a final third year of novitiate usually done after the completion of a Jesuit's clerical studies—at a house the Society owned near Saint Mary Major. In the same letter the newly ordained priest added: "After that what shall I do? I do not want to tell you about that now and then have everything changed, hence it is not well to say too much. . . ."[15]

The secret that he had apparently been nourishing for a long time was an ardent desire to serve God in the foreign missions of North America. Whether this desire came as a result of reading De Smet's *Letters and Sketches,* or in reply to Father General Roothaan's appeal for volunteers for the Oregon Mission, we do not know. Whatever the reason, Providence did not delay in fulfilling his wishes in a series of happenings deplorable from a human standpoint, but ultimately with happy results for the young Jesuit.

Early in 1848 the Italian revolutionaries were able to obtain from the King, Charles Albert, the dissolution of the Jesuits throughout his States. Shortly thereafter the Italian Jesuits were obliged to scatter. A goodly number of them, natives of Savoy and clad as diocesan priests or in lay attire, followed the Aosta Valley and then over the Petit-Saint-Bernard pass to Moûtiers. Others, like Father Miege, went to the port of Rome at Civitavecchia and thence to Marseilles by ship. Arriving at Marseilles, Father Miege paid a visit to Father Roothaan, who had arrived there several days before.[16] It was Father Roothaan who gave him permission to go to the missions in North America.

Father Miege then set out for a brief visit with his family in Savoy. Going first to the major seminary of Moûtiers, he caused a commotion that eventually ended in peals of laughter among students and faculty. It seems that while students and faculty were at high Mass on Easter Monday morning, they left one of the servants to guard the house. Up came a tall figure with a big beard and an imposing presence who asked to see Father Lanchet, the professor of dogma. The servant was convinced that this was one of those "terrible, voracious creatures" so feared at the time. Accordingly, he closed and barred the door and armed himself with a loaded musket. When the seminarians returned from Mass the servant excitedly told them how courageous he had been in the midst of all the danger. Meanwhile, Father Miege went to visit his brother Urban whom he had not seen for many years. He told him about the "charming" reception he had received at the seminary, and after a brief rest, the two brothers went to restore calm and peace there. That the porter should have mistaken Miege for some ruffian who apparently was terrorizing the area led to many moments of entertainment.[17]

John Baptist had only a few days to visit with his family, which included his venerable old mother whom he loved so dearly, his brothers, and his nephews and nieces in whom he had so loving an interest—six of whom, incidentally, were later called to the religious life. His was a closely knit family, and it was not easy to leave them for far-distant America. While making the Spiritual Exercises of Saint Ignatius during his noviceship at Milan, he had come to know Christ as his king, and he had promised to follow him as best he could. Later, as a more experienced religious, he had asked to be sent to the American missions. His request was granted, and he was "missioned" accordingly. Miege was not one to look backward once he had put his hand to the plow.

3

TO THE AMERICAN MISSIONS

On June 1, 1848, together with forty-three fellow Jesuits, John Baptist boarded the sailing vessel *Providence*. Since the *Providence* had been used for cargo only, "accommodations" had to be set up for the voyagers in the hold. The captain did not seem too competent; the crew was not reliable; and on leaving Antwerp a drunken pilot almost ran the vessel on a rock. Years later one of the Jesuit travelers, Father Burchard Villiger, noted that: "After leaving Antwerp, we were to have reached New York in four weeks. It took seven weeks with many storms, bad accommodations, scarcity of food, suffering from hunger and thirst, so much so that, on arriving at the quarantine in New York, we rejoiced at getting boiled potatoes; we looked upon it as a feast of the first class."[1] Villiger does not mention that the mainmast was swept away in one of the storms. One could scarcely blame most of the crew for deserting the vessel immediately, once New York was reached at high noon on July 19.

Of the newly arrived Jesuits only one stayed in New York. Eighteen left a few days later for stations in the Maryland province of the Society, and the rest left by "fast mail train" for St. Louis, Missouri, via Cincinnati. Among the latter was Father Miege. Years later the bishop related with laughter and delight an experience the group had in Philadelphia. Wishing to travel further by boat, they asked where they could find a "vapor," literally translating *vapeur,* the French word for steamer. A crowd gathered around them, some laughing, some trying to understand what they were saying, and everybody out talking one another, until one man pointed down a street. Following his directions they eventually found a steamer.[2]

One has to remember that in the midnineteenth century English was not as commonly spoken throughout the world as it is today. French was the language of the courts. The Jesuits, having to leave home in such a hurry, would scarcely have had time to pick up more than a smattering of English. The surprising thing is that they came to speak and write their adopted language so well, as is testified by their "relations" and other writings. A good example of how hard they struggled to obtain a working knowledge is the case of the noble-born Paul Ponziglione. In 1850 he was sent to Saint Joseph's College, in Bardstown, Kentucky, to study English. In an effort to correct his faulty pronunciation, he asked for permission to read to his confreres in the refectory during meals. Since the spelling and the pronunciation of the English language are not always in accord, he afforded the community considerable merriment over his blunders. Still, we are told that no one enjoyed this merriment more than he himself did.[3]

When, after considerable trouble, the little group finally reached St. Louis, Missouri, in the fall of 1848, they were assigned various positions and places of residence. Father Miege's first assignment was to the assistant pastorship of the now historical little church of Saint Charles, Missouri. He made his residence there with two Jesuit priests and two brothers. Twice a week he went to Portage of the Sioux, a mission of which he had charge. His flock at Portage consisted of what Miege considered "good" and "peaceful" natives among whom he experienced a great deal of consolation. However, his mission there was not without its problems. For one thing, he suffered considerably from the elements. He found himself unaccustomed to the rigors of cold and ice and snow during the long winter months. Moreover, inundations in this raw river country were sudden and frequent, and means of communication were primitive. His existence was not only difficult, it was frequently quite dangerous.

In April 1849, his superiors called him to St. Louis to accompany Father Ignatius Maes and to get to know the Winnebagos, an Indian tribe living near the source of the Mississippi River. The two missionaries boarded ship at St. Louis and went up river as far as St. Paul. John Baptist was quite surprised at the luxury of the *Saint Peter,* a steamer on which the missionaries traveled. He told his brother that traveling on an American steamer was like being in a small floating chateau with its richly appointed salon, its little private cabin where one could get rest, its balconies on which to contemplate the sky and water, and its promenade deck to walk and breathe in the freshness of the night air. He hastened to add that, though it may not have seemed to be a fitting way for missionaries to travel, the cost was only forty francs compared with one hundred francs for land travel.[4]

The two Fathers left the boat at St. Paul and continued their trip by wagon. Father Miege set down a very interesting account of his trip in a letter to his brother Urban. The Mississippi impressed him profoundly. He wrote: "To all the magnificence of this enormous mass, which does not stop growing until it loses itself in the Ocean, one has to add the impression produced by the truly magnificent spectacle of these immense forests which border the Mississippi to its mouth at New Orleans, and whose gigantic trees have no other enemies outside their age and the sudden broadening of the river that borders them."[5] Father Miege was awed by the Mississippi with its "frightful urge to increase its domain," gradually eating away at its banks and carrying everything along—trees, lands, and even houses. He mentioned it was because of this that the towns on the river were "set up against hills and placed where the height of the banks" protected them against flash floods. He was surprised to note the rapidity with which these river towns were growing and attributed this growth to the industry of the American people and a vast influx of European emigrants. Father Miege visited a number of these towns, which were for the most part only ten years old but already had five thousand, six thousand, and even ten thousand inhabitants. He considered the most remarkable of these to be Allon (Alton?), Annibal (Hannibal), and Naavoo (Nauvoo), the latter an early settlement of Mormons and French Socialists.[6]

After Nauvoo, Miege then visited Bartington (not on a modern map), Rock Island, and Galena, where he arrived "after a two-or three-hour ascent of the river of fevers, so called because of the unhealthy air of its swampy banks." He found Dubuque to be a "lovely little town" surrounded by hills rich in lead mines. He predicted that the advantage of its position would soon make it "one of the important commercial centers on the Mississippi." The major drawback, he felt, would be the difficulty of boats docking at low water. In that case the landing facilities of Galena, a few leagues downriver, might be preferred. At Dubuque, Father Miege obtained valuable information on the Native Americans he was supposed to visit. He also received a copy of a catechism translated into Sioux and printed by a Father Ravou, as well as part of a bible in Sioux printed by Methodist missionaries.[7]

Fathers Miege and Maes, accompanied by Father Ravou, left Dubuque on April 25 to board the *Cora,* which Miege described as "a nice little steamboat, whose elegance, together with the cordial amiability of its captain, M. Gorman, left nothing to be desired by even the most demanding traveler." Moving upstream, about the only thing they encountered on either side of the river was a few scattered dwellings of ten, fifteen, or twenty families. After three days, the *Cora* arrived at St. Paul, "a small town" begun two or three years before, which already counted "nearly 1,000 inhabitants, almost all Canadian." Since it was still night, instead of landing in the darkness, the party moved up to Fort Saint-Pierre. Actually, this was not much more than a stronghold intended "to hold the Sioux in deference and to facilitate commerce with them." Since steamboats could not advance farther up the river because of the cascades, the *Cora* returned to St. Paul after stopping for a few hours of rest for the passengers. Meanwhile, Father Ravou stayed on at the fort.[8]

The distance from St. Paul to the proposed end of their journey, about 150 miles, had to be made by land, either on horseback or in a wagon. The cost of a riding horse was about $3.00 a day. Since they had fifteen hundred pounds of luggage, the two Fathers decided on a wagon and two horses, for which they had to pay $32.00 for twelve days. On Monday evening, April 30, perched on top of a pile of trunks and sacks, they set out on the road toward the Winnebagos "across the immense prairies of the upper Mississippi." After four hours of travel they sought respite for the night, since by this time it was quite late. They stopped at the Cascades of Saint Antoine. Father Miege explained to his brother how "the whole enormous mass of the Mississippi, confined here in a very narrow channel, falls 25 feet." He felt that the fall would be even more spectacular if the rock, which gave rise to the cascade, were more perpendicular. However, it still made such an impression on him that he felt himself unable to give an adequate description.[9]

The next morning the travelers set out again and in forty hours arrived at the *Rapides des Sacs* (Sauk Rapids above St. Cloud). At the Rapides they found almost six hundred members of the Winnebago tribe. Close by was the government agent with whom they had to make arrangements. Although the agent showed the priests sufficient goodwill, he was not too encouraging. It seems that the part of the tribe that had asked Washington, D.C., for "black robes" was camped on government property. The government insisted that the remainder of the tribe join their brothers at Long Prairie, where they had settled under the guidance of a Presbyterian minister. The Fathers accordingly asked for a meeting of the Council of Chiefs. At the meeting the agent spoke first. He pointed out that their "grandfather"—that is, the president of the United States—also wanted them to join the rest of the tribe. Finally, he warned that if they "did not want to be reasonable, he would be obliged to refuse them their provisions and money."[10]

While the agent was speaking, the high chief Wanschik had been puffing on a four-foot long pipe. Now he solemnly rose, touched the hand of the agent and then those of the two Black Robes, and stepped into the center of a circle. There followed, as Father Miege told his brother, "a speech with as much ardor as your Piedmontese Chambers produce when they want to make war against Austria." As interpreted the speech went as follows:

> The intention of our Grandfather is that we be happy, that we have lots of fish, good hunting, and good lands; there is nothing of all this in the place where you wish to send us. Our Grandfather cannot want to send us there; we will not go. We are happy to see the Black Robes we

asked for and we will tell them in a few days where they should build their house. If you refuse us the provisions and the money you owe us, you will do nothing except to rob us as you have done up to the present.[11]

Two other chiefs spoke in much the same manner.

Father Miege was beginning to be concerned, since he was due back at St. Louis on May 10, 1849, and the whole situation remained most uncertain. Hence it was that the two Fathers decided to go to Long Prairie, some seventy miles north, to see the country for themselves. They left on May 3 and, after two days of travel "by a frightful road, through woods and marshes," arrived on May 5. There they found "a poor little plain, wild, sandy and sterile, between forests and marshes, offering nothing to cheer, nothing to revive hearts oppressed by the chagrin of an exile. . . . " A hundred or so lodges were afflicted by scurvy, contracted from tainted meat they had been given throughout the winter. At the same time, some sixty Catholic half-breeds received them graciously and encouraged them to stay.[12]

Arriving back in St. Louis on May 15, Father Miege was given a commission similar to the assignment just completed. This time he was to go up the Missouri River for thirty-five days to visit the natives there; he would then go back downriver to Fort Pierre, where he would pick up an interpreter, a guide, and horses to visit the various Sioux tribes in the area. However, due to a serious cholera epidemic, the trip was postponed for several days. It was abandoned completely when a terrible fire broke out in St. Louis and destroyed countless warehouses and twenty-three steamboats docked along the wharves. The boat on which Father Miege was supposed to have traveled, together with its $50,000 worth of merchandise, was destroyed.[13]

Cholera was raging in the mission when Father Miege had left in April. Since there was nobody to care for the people on a regular basis, he returned and remained there for two or three months of what turned out to be "a continual race, day and night." One of his companions contracted cholera, but fortunately recovered; a second was struck down by sheer fatigue. Father Miege himself caught a fever, although it only lasted one week.

In September 1849, much to his regret—he was, after all,
devoted to mission work—he was called to assume a much
more tranquil position at Florissant, then the novitiate and
house of studies of the Missouri province. There he was
socius or assistant to the Father Rector, where he served as
minister—buyer; manager—for the members of the house. In
addition, he taught moral theology to the young Jesuits who
resided there. Further, he was preparing for his final examination in theology, which he could not take in Rome because of
the troubles at the time.[14]

John Baptist was rapidly becoming Americanized. In 1850,
for example, he wrote to Urban: "You are going to laugh
when I tell you that I am a staunch republican, but as one is
in America . . . . Here everybody thinks, does, writes, speaks,
eats, and acts as he wishes. Be you Catholic, Presbyterian,
Methodist, Anabaptist, Mormon, socialist, etc., even to be seen
as a Jesuit and recognized as such, nobody will insult you,
nobody will outlaw you, for the very simple reason that you
are free and that the law protects you as such."[15]

There is a bit of confusion as to Miege's whereabouts at the
time. Ponziglione would seem to unravel the puzzle when he
tells us that: "From the fall of 1849 to the spring of 1851
Father John B. Miege was for a while taking care of our
Church of S. Charles Missouri, and the balance of the time he
was teaching moral theology to our Scholastics in Florissant."[16]
This solution fits in better with the descriptions in the Missouri
province catalogs of 1849 and 1850. What happened after
those dates John Baptist tells us himself. In a letter to Urban
in November 1850, after a beautiful eulogy to his mother who
had just passed away and a reference to having passed his
final examination in theology, he admits that "since September
he has been a resident at St. Louis University. There he was
teaching moral theology and French rhetoric. He was engaged
in some prefecting, some spiritual counseling, an exhortation
in English every 15 days, a talk in French each month to a
French society of which he was president . . . without stating
the rest."[17] It was at St. Louis University in the fall of 1850 that
he first learned about the possibility of becoming a bishop.

In a sense the story started a year earlier, in 1849, when the
Seventh Provincial Council of Baltimore petitioned Pius IX to
erect a vicariate in the Indian Territory, which at the time

Map of the West, 1854. Bishop Miege's original
diocese is shown in heavy lines. Today, this area
comprises three archdioceses and roughly twelve
dioceses. Reprinted from *The Jesuit Bulletin* 35, no.
4 (August 1956): 9.

stretched from the Missouri border in the east to the Rocky
Mountains in the west and from the Canadian border on the
north to New Mexico on the south. The names of three
Missouri province Jesuits—Fathers John Bax, Francis X. De
Coen, and Miege—were submitted to the Holy Father. "The
bishops in council," Father John Elet informed Father General
Roothaan, "have resolved to propose one of our Fathers to
the Holy See as a future vicar-apostolic. Father De Smet was
proposed, but I answered that he would not suit. The
Archbishop of St. Louis [Peter Kenrick] then spoke to me of
Father Miege and I answered that he would suit, but that I
thought it my duty to refrain from pronouncing for or against
the measure."[18]

Father General Roothaan, writing to Cardinal Fransoni,
Prefect of the Propaganda, said, in effect, that he had no
objections to a Jesuit being made bishop of a true mission territory but that the proposed vicariate did not seem to fit that
category, judging from the way that white men were entering
the Indian Territory. The more white men that entered the
Territory, especially after the Kansas-Nebraska Act of 1854
when the area was opened to whites, the more the Indian set-

tlements and, hence, the missions would become disrupted. But the Jesuits, by rule and by custom, did not favor acting as bishops of dioceses peopled by ordinary Catholics. Father Miege, for example, came to America to administer to Indians, not to white settlers. (Today there are only 431 Indians in the state of Kansas). The Father General had mentioned how the once flourishing mission at Saint Mary's among the Flatheads was already in dire straits because of the white men. At the same time Father De Smet wrote to assure the Father General that no harm could come to the Society by accepting "a forlorn vicariate in the wilderness of the American West." If a Jesuit must be chosen for the position, the general told the cardinal, Father Miege would be suitable.[19]

Meanwhile, almost everybody at the university seems to have known what was "in the air" except the future bishop himself. As the story is told, one evening on returning to the study hall, Father Miege found a package on his desk. Thinking it to be a practical joke of some kind, he took it to his room and left it unopened. Three days later, when the Father Rector told him that it contained his appointment as vicar apostolic of the Indian Territory, he was severely disturbed and "firmly but respectfully" returned the package to its sender.[20] In a letter to Archbishop Samuel Eccleston of Baltimore, he wrote: "I received from Baltimore on October 12, 1850, bulls which appointed me Vicar Apostolic of that part of the Indian Territory which lies to the East of the Rocky Mountains. After having seriously examined the matter before God, I considered myself obliged in conscience to refuse a dignity which I see clearly to be beyond my physical and moral strength. In returning the bulls to His Eminence Cardinal Fransoni, I gave him at the same time the well grounded reasons for my refusal. I am convinced that his eminence will recognize the justice of my decision and will set aside the proposal. . . ."[21]

Actually Father Miege sent the bulls to the Father General asking him to return them to the cardinal. We gather how distressed he really was from his letter to Father Roothaan. In return, Roothan sympathized with him and reminded him that since he had not yet made his final profession he was not bound to refuse the dignity. He had acted in the spirit of his vocation. Moreover, nothing in the bulls *demanded* that he accept it. The Father General, however, seemed to believe that the affair was not thus easily resolved, since he advised the young Jesuit to "await the issue in peace and pray with confidence in our Lord."[22]

Meanwhile, John Baptist wrote to Urban to explain what was happening. "While I was thus almost drowned in these troublous details," he began, referring to his work at the university, "something happened to me that I want to tell you about on the condition that you tell nobody unless it is already known. It is unique enough to allow you to laugh over it. *I have just missed being made a bishop!* On October 12 I found a large package on my desk coming from the Propaganda; it contained bulls, letters, provisions for the erection of a Vicariate Apostolic for the Indian Territory east of the Rocky Mountains; and your poor brother was named bishop of Messana *in partibus infidelium.* I did scarcely more than glance at the documents. On reading the address: To Monsignor J. Miege, etc. I fully realized the suspicion that bothered me for several months. I opened the package simply to see if it included any *express orders* to accept. Since it contained only a simple nomination, I closed the whole thing up again and sent the package back to Propaganda, protesting that I would never accept such a burden, and the reasons for my refusal are such that I firmly trust that they will leave me in peace in this matter. I would a thousand times rather return to Europe than accept this dignity. I have enough difficulty keeping myself out of trouble when I have only myself to guide, what would it be if I had to guide others?"[23]

Father Roothaan wrote to Cardinal Barnabo, secretary of the Congregation, stating the reasons for Father Miege's unwillingness to accept the appointment. In return, writing on December 11, 1850, the cardinal informed the general that Pius IX "ordered [Miege] to be given an absolute precept of obedience to accept the charge laid upon him."[24] Father Roothaan then sent a consoling letter to Miege. "What I gave you grounds for suspecting has actually happened," he wrote. "The Holy Father has expressed his formal, absolute wish that you accept the vicariate-apostolic with the episcopal character. Here, then, is the precept, the will of God. The Briefs which you sent back are returning to you—there is nothing for you to say. Submit and pray and think only of the manner in which you must conduct yourself in this new charge, *ad majorem Dei gloriam.*"

Roothaan then pointed out the consoling side of the situation, explaining that John Baptist would remain a member of the Society and that it might all work out for the good of the missions, particularly west of the Rockies, where the Society was in danger of losing the chance of doing missionary work there. "Courage, then, my dear Father, and confidence in God and His holy Mother!" Roothaan then added some fatherly advice concerning his conduct as a bishop and ended by saying that five thousand francs had been placed in his account with the procurator in Paris.[25]

About the same time that John Baptist received the letter from Father Roothaan, he heard from his old friend Father Gailland at Saint Mary's Mission in Kansas. He congratulated him and then, explaining all the wonderful advantages of the mission, he extended a cordial invitation to the bishop-elect to make his headquarters there. Gailland wrote:

It is with sentiments of profound joy that we have come to learn of your nomination to the Vicariate Apostolic of the Indian Territory this side of the Rocky Mountains. Father De Smet informed us of this happy news and the American papers have already announced it in their columns. . . . I have informed our Indians that the greatest of all the Black Robes was going to send a great Black Robe to provide for the salvation of all the Indians this side of the great Mountain; that this great Robe would probably not delay long to visit them. This news filled their hearts with joy. They look for his first appearance at the beginning of next spring on their return from the big hunt. A very large number of them have not been confirmed; they are impatiently waiting to receive the fullness of the gifts of the Holy Spirit; we shall profit at the same time by this circumstance to have the three churches blessed which we have already built and a fourth which we will likely build at another location.

The Potawatomies as well as all of our Fathers and Brothers are firmly convinced that this will be the See of the Vicar Apostolic of the Indians. What gives rise to this conviction is that the Nation of the Potawatomies counts in its midst a numerous and fervent body of Christians; being the first Indians of the Vicariate to embrace christianity, they are tempted to believe that they have the right to this preference. There is here a small community of Ours and a community of the Ladies of the Sacred Heart of Jesus with two classroom buildings, one for boys, the other for girls. At the headquarters of the Mission stands a church which, without being comparable to the beautiful churches of Europe, nevertheless deserves a name among the churches already built or to be built in the Indian Territory. One of our Coadjutor brothers here has made an altar remarkable for its beauty in this Native Land.

Furthermore, this place is, so to speak, the center of the Vicariate. From here it will be easy to make apostolic journeys to all the Indian nations of the Vicariate. On one side are situated the numerous nations of the Sioux, that of the Pawnies, the Iowa, the Kickapoux, the Delawares, the Shawnies, the Sacs, the Foxes, the Kansas, the Miamies, the Peorias, the Ottawas, the Osages, etc. Some of these people can be reached in a day's journey by horseback; in three or four days one can reach the flourishing Mission of the Osages. Add to this that once one gets to know the language of the Potawatomies, he can easily converse with the Sacs, the Foxes, the Kickapoux, the Ottawas, and, after a bit of work, with the Miamis, the Peorias, and the Piankishaws: after a bit of study the Pastor would have the advantage of being able to converse directly with his flocks of diverse peoples.

Finally, after telling Father Miege how the Indians in the area had urgently requested assistance from the Black Robes, and how much good could be done, Gailland concludes:

To those who pretend that we can do practically no good among the Indians, we answer: before pronouncing such a judgement, taste and see, *gustate et videte;* meditate on that saying of St. Ignatius, inscribed on each page of the institute, *Ad majorem Dei gloriam,* and then say if our Saintly founder did not embrace in his zeal savage as well as civilized peoples.[26]

A month before his consecration, the bishop-elect wrote to his brother Urban:

The same post that brought your last letter also brought me one from Reverend Father General, who settled the miserable affair I mentioned to you. He told me that the Holy Father expressed his formal, absolute wish that I accept this Vicariate Apostolic together with the dignity of the bishopric. All that I can tell you about this matter is that the good God seems to me to have me pay back the numerous debts I have contracted against his divine goodness. Since you sincerely wish for my well-being and all that can guarantee it, you must frequently beg Our Lord and the most Blessed Virgin to grant super-abundant grace where the responsibility lies and where the misery is the deepest. Truly I did not come to America for this kind of tribulation, and if I had been able to suspect the slightest possibility of it, I would never have left a country where I was better known and as a consequence sheltered from this heavy burden.[27]

In reply, Urban made every effort to encourage his brother to enter his new career with confidence. At the same time he joked about his newly gained dignity, his future cathedral, his coming chapter, and so on. The letter seems to have cheered John Baptist since, writing to Urban on the eve of his conse-cration, he declared: "I received your letter of February 14 on the 16 of March; it did me good, and I laughed for the first time, I think, in three months. I trust that the good God and the Blessed Virgin will keep me. Let us hope that I have the good fortune to save my soul, and to help as much as possi-ble these poor Indians to get to know our holy religion, for the rest may the will of God be done. . . ."[28]

Father John Baptist Miege was consecrated bishop on March 25, 1851, in Saint Francis Xavier Church in St. Louis by Archbishop Peter Kenrick assisted by Bishops James Van de Velde and Maurice de St. Palais. Writing some years later, Thomas Ambrose Butler reported that when all the dignitaries were gathered and ready to begin the ceremony there was no Father Miege. After a somewhat lengthy search he was discov-ered kneeling in his room, bathed in tears.[29]

4

THE BISHOP ENTERS HIS VICARIATE

Before setting out for Kansas, John Baptist informed his brother Urban of his appointment as vicar apostolic and mentioned that he would leave for his mission after Easter. He would be accompanied by Father De Smet "who knew these wild lands very well and who has time and again visited the uncivilized nations who inhabit them." The plan was first to visit the Potawatomi where three of the Jesuit Fathers (John Duerinck, Christian Hoecken, and Maurice Gailland) and three brothers (Andrew Mazella, Daniel Doneen, and John Dugan), had already established a mission for some three thousand Native Americans. The mission had a school for boys conducted by a brother and one for girls conducted by the Sisters of the Sacred Heart. The bishop would then proceed to the Osage Mission, which had been founded by the Jesuits a few years before. Fathers Andrew Ehrensberger and John Baptist Goeldlin, assisted by Brother Joseph Prassnegg, conducted this mission. Here, too, there were schools for boys and girls, the latter being cared for by the Sisters of Loretto. The bishop's plan was to visit the tribes of the interior in an attempt to ascertain their mood.[1] These were remnants of tribes which, in the course of the years, had been partly destroyed by wars and partly by that terrible enemy of the natives, smallpox. They were scattered far to the north and to the Texas border in the south.[2]

John Baptist knew what he was facing. He mentioned to his brother the many dangers that lay ahead. Although food and lodging eventually materialized, he noted that in the course of the journeys "one recites frequently enough and with feeling the words of the Our Father that speak of daily bread."[3]

When the time arrived for Bishop Miege to leave St. Louis, it was not Father De Smet but Father Paul Ponziglione who accompanied him. Father Paul, as he was called, had been studying English and helping out at the Saint Joseph's Jesuit College and Parish in Bardstown, Kentucky. He asked the father provincial for and was granted permission to accompany his old friend Father Miege. In turn, 1851 marked the beginning for him of a long and fruitful career in the mission fields of Kansas.[4]

After a tedious, week-long journey by boat up the Missouri, the party arrived at St. Joseph, Missouri, on May 24. After four days they crossed the river and headed for Saint Mary's, the bishop's first residence in the western grasslands.[5] There were six persons in the party: Bishop Miege, Father Paul, Brother Sebastian Schlienger, Brother Patrick Phelan—still a novice in the Society—and two Creoles. Fathers Miege and Ponziglione led the procession on horseback. The brothers and the two Creole teamsters followed with wagons laden with furniture and provisions for the missions.[6]

Anyone who has lived in Kansas for any length of time knows what terrible storms can come rolling off the prairies on occasion. It was such a storm that hit the little party on its very first day out. Father Ponziglione tells the story:

> About 2 o'clock P.M. the clouds began to gather over our head, the wind began to blow a tempest, lightning and thunderclaps succeeded themselves rapidly, and at 3 o'clock P.M. a heavy rain began to pour down. As there was no way to reach any shelter, we kept on taking matters as safely as we could, yet the prospect was very gloomy, and we thought better to recite some prayers. At the suggestion of Father Miege we said the Memorare, and hardly had got through with it, when lightning struck the ground so close to us, that we felt as if a log had struck us in a slanting way over our head.

Our horses seemed to have been affected by it worse than we were, for both stumbled to the ground. But as they soon got up again, we continued our journey apparently with a stoical indifference, but I assure you that in our heart we felt a little uneasy not knowing what might come next, and so went on repeating the Memorare more fervently than ever before.[7]

In spite of the storm the party kept plodding along, until shortly before dark when they stopped for the night. The spot these "tenderfeet" chose for a camp on the top of the prairie was not too good, since there was not even a stump, let alone a tree, to tie up their horses. The animals grazed in the lush grass, where they were less likely to wander off. There was no question of a fire since there was no wood. Rather, the wayfarers took out some bread and dry meat and, as Father Paul wrote, "like the Jews of old standing with staff in hand and hat on head" ate their supper. They did not lack fresh drinking water—the rain kept coming down. Fortunately, the bishop was able to use the four chairs that he brought with him to adorn his "palace," so that the party did not have to sleep in water that flowed "a half-foot deep" round about. There they sat praying, singing, reciting rhymes, eating, and trying to sleep. Wet through and through, cold, worn out with fatigue, teeth chattering, with visions of fever and stomach cramps, they "enjoyed" a miserable night. At daybreak the rain stopped, the clouds scattered, and a radiant sun emerged.[8] After a bit of moving about they all found themselves to be in perfect health.

Everybody was happy until they glanced at the bishop. Noticing that he seemed quite perplexed, Father Paul asked him whether he was unwell. "Oh no," he answered, "but don't you hear?" Suddenly the two Creoles burst out laughing and told the others that the noise was that of grazing prairie chickens. The good bishop had mistaken the cooing of the chickens for the voices of hostile Indians about to attack the party. Once his suspicions were relieved, he took his shotgun and went after the fowl. In a matter of minutes he returned with four fat chickens—as nice a breakfast as they could wish for. After two days on the road the party reached Saint Mary's Mission at noon on May 31.[9]

The story of how the Potawatomi came to be settled at Saint Mary's is extremely complex. Justice cannot be done by a brief narrative. Yet the story has been told at length by others. Here let us simply point out that the policy of the federal government to remove the Indian tribes east of the Mississippi River into the Indian Territory was being fully implemented by the 1830s. The United States had always considered Indian claims to possession of their lands to be sound. Hence, Indian titles could only be extinguished by voluntary cession alone. Throughout the United States countless such treaties of cession took place. Between 1795 and 1833 fifty-four transfers of land occurred in Indiana alone.[10] Unfortunately, as the white settlers moved in ever-increasing numbers into the Midwest, they ruined the hunting lands upon which the Indians depended for food, clothing, and shelter. The whites, so very desirous of the land, could not understand why such a comparatively small number of Native Americans could claim such boundless acres. Moreover, the Indians, with tribal laws of their own, could not always grasp the reason for obeying state laws. Then, too, there was the matter of liquor and other corrupting influences of the whites, so that even good people, sympathetic toward the Indian cause, favored an isolationist program.

Although the Potawatomi of Michigan, Indiana, and Illinois emigrated westward in numerous groups, by the summer of 1838 there were two main tribes—the Prairie band at Council Bluffs, Iowa, and the Forest Potawatomi, of whom many lived, for a while at least, in Sugar Creek, Kansas. Meanwhile, as early as 1825, the Indian agent, General George Rogers Clark, had asked the Jesuits of the Missouri province for members to establish a mission among the Kansas Indians. Beginning in 1833, Father Benedict Roux, S.J., visited the Kickapoos, who dwelt along the Missouri River in the vicinity of Fort Leavenworth. It was in the Kickapoo village, in 1836, that the first Catholic church in what is now the state of Kansas was built for Saint Francis Xavier Mission. The mission had been founded the same year by Father Charles Van Quickenborne, S.J.[11]

When, in 1848, the Potawatomi all joined together to form a unified Potawatomi Nation, Saint Mary's Mission on the Kansas (Kaw) River came to be the dwelling of the Catholic population. Meanwhile, in 1847, a second mission had been

Bishop Miege's first "cathedral," Potawatomi
Mission, Saint Mary's, Kansas, circa 1851. Source
unknown.

established among the Osage tribe, some sixty miles directly
south of present-day Topeka. On these two missions depended several other stations among the Kickapoos, Miamis,
Piankeshaws, Weas, Peorias, and Quapaws. The total Catholic
population was about six thousand. Such was the situation
when Bishop Miege first came to Kansas.[12]

Apparently the Potawatomi at Saint Mary's were expecting
the bishop, since they had grouped at various points along
the way. As soon as they spotted the arrivals they ran to the
mission to notify the Fathers. Together with a number of
natives, the Fathers then went in procession for about a mile
to welcome the bishop and bring him to the village. They all
knelt down to receive his blessing and then escorted him to
the church. After praying, the bishop emerged from the structure and was greeted by still more cheers. Finally, as Father
Paul tells us, they followed him "to his episcopal palace,
which consisted of a poor log cabin, a little longer than a very
common shanty."[13]

A more formal reception for Bishop Miege took place the
next morning. Father Gailland tells the story:

> Early in the morning . . . the Indians, men and women,
> filled our mission yard, and were very anxious to
> show their high consideration for the great Black-
> gown. The women were on foot, carrying on their shoul-
> ders their squealing babies, wrapped up in red, green or

blue blankets. The men were on horseback. At the fixed time the procession began towards the church, headed by the choir-boys, followed by the acolytes and clergymen, with the Bishop. The Indians in their cavalcade, by quick and precise evolutions representing a variety of figures, displayed a grand and attractive spectacle. The singing of the choir, the frequent discharge of musketry by the soldiers, the modesty and piety of the neophytes added to the solemnity of the ceremony.[14]

Judging from a letter written shortly afterward, the bishop seems to have been particularly delighted with the accoutrement of the Indians:

About eight o'clock in the morning, the cavalry, banners in hand, gathered a short distance from the church under the command of one of the chiefs of the Nation or Tribe. The uniform of this brave imitated quite well that of a marshal of France but in dimensions much more majestic and solemn; for in addition to a sword worn in the manner of Henry IV, his cocked hat, made of pasteboard covered with red, yellow and white paper, was certainly the longest and highest affair of its kind that I have ever seen; at the center was a white cross a good foot high. The whole was topped with a plume having a thick stem, weighed down with wild turkey feathers.

The dress of the subaltern militia was somewhat less chivalrous, however there was much to admire. The military band, consisting of a violin and a drum, was preceded by a drum major who had for a shako nothing less than a large piece of buffalo skin styled in the form of the shakos of our European drum majors in full uniform. Next came the infantry armed with carbines and dressed in full Indian splendor. Hence there were coats for all seasons, of all styles, of all colors, the same for shoes; shirts of many colors; short trousers rich in ribbons as well as patches; finally a sort of turban covered in part with long tufts of black hair, which gave a quite savage expression to the sunken eyes and the copper-colored faces of my good diocesans. Add to all this a prodigious quantity of ribbons and yellow and red handkerchiefs attached or sewn a bit on all sides, and you will have some strokes, ill drawn of an interesting reality.[15]

The church, which could hold from five to six hundred persons, was packed, Miege added—weapons were left at the door and horses were tied to rails in the yard. All these good folk assisted at Mass with a piety and devotion he had never seen before. After the Mass there was more parading, processions, music, and discharge of musketry, which was followed by a feast featuring a six-hundred-pound steer, lots of bread, sugar, and coffee.[16]

The bishop did not waste much time in feasting. After resting for a few days, he was up and about and, like any missionary priest, he spent his time teaching catechism, preaching, visiting the sick, administering the sacraments, and, in general, trying to make himself useful.

Bishop Miege remained at Saint Mary's for about one month and then, on June 23, set out for the Osage Mission. He was accompanied by Fathers Ponziglione and Duerinck, Brother Patrick Phelan, and an Indian guide. All rode horseback, each with a blanket to keep warm and to serve as a bed at night. They had enough food to last four days. They reached their destination on June 26, to be "most kindly received" by Fathers John Schoenmakers and John Bax and Father Theodore Hermann, a diocesan priest who taught the boys of the mission.[17] News of the bishop's arrival soon spread, and the next morning John Baptist received his second lesson in Indian eloquence. Father Paul tells us how it came about:

> The great Chief of the Osages, George White Hair . . . in company of his Braves all painted in the most grotesque form came to pay an official visit to our Bishop. After the usual courteous greetings, and I might say parliamentary talk, George White Hair stood up, and bowing with great gravity to Bishop Miege asked him by interpreter whether he was the Great Priest, and the Head Chief of all the Black-gowns that were in the Indian country? Our Bishop answered that he was. Then the Chief replied "O Great Priest, and Head Chief of all the Black-gown listen

to us thy Children! When a few a years ago a Black-gown [Father Peter De Smet] came here from St. Louis to visit us, he gave us a steer to feast, and as we were asking him to give us another one, he told us that he was only an ordinary Black-gown, but "when," said he, "the Great Priest, the Head Chief of all the Black-gown that are in the Indian country will come to visit you, he will give you Seven Steers. Now as you say that you are the Great Priest and the Head Chief of all the Black-gowns, so we want you to be good towards your poor Children and give us the Seven Steers.[18]

Father Miege was surprised at the "ingenuity and subtility" of George White Hair's argument, and he laughed "very freely" at its conclusion. Then, turning to Father Schoenmakers, an experienced missionary, he asked him what was to be done. "Tell the Chief," came the reply, "that he will get his seven steers." The Osages were overjoyed at learning that their petition was being granted. Father Paul tells us that they all stood up, crying " *'Owe Owe! Tan-he! Tapuska Whatanca,'* which means "Joy, Joy! This is good! O Great Priest!" and as this seemed to have been the principal object of their visit, off they went to look for the Steers, and for several days they had a great time, eating, drinking, singing and dancing war dances in honor of our bishop." Bishop Miege stayed at the Osage Mission for about a month. Then, leaving Father Ponziglione and Brother Phelan there, he returned to Saint Mary's.

In short order the bishop came to love the Potawatomi, of whom fifteen hundred were Catholic. On one occasion he wrote of them:

They attend mass daily, and approach the sacraments in great numbers each week, all of them at least each month; they practice with admirable fervor all the other pious exercises the Church has established to increase the devotion of her children. It is indeed touching to see, on fine summer evenings, good people gather in large numbers in the center of the village to recite together the rosary, and then sing in their own language hymns in honor of the Blessed Virgin. I do not think that I have ever experienced such delightful emotions than those which made my heart beat the first time I heard, in our wilderness, these natives sing so loudly and with such heartfelt devotion the praises of our Mother.[19]

Unfortunately things were not so lovely in some other villages and in a nearby settlement of mixed bloods. Miege characterized the latter as "immoral, drunkards, liars all, deaf to all instruction, and of such rude impiety as must necessarily give rise to this singular mixture of the worst passions."[20]

His opinion of the Osages, whom he visited a bit later, was not much better. While he thought them to be perhaps "the handsomest race of men in the whole Indian country, six feet tall, with robust, well-formed bodies," he considered their souls to be "the reservoir of all evil human passions." He saw them as "thieving, lazy, drunken, debauched, proud" and added, in effect, that one could call them what one wanted without fear of maligning them.[21]

Still, the Jesuits who worked with the Osage tribes were committed to them, as was their bishop. The Fathers kept visiting them, wandering through their camps, teaching them in private as well as in public.[22] In a sense, the results were disappointing since there were few baptisms among the adults. However, as the *Annual Report* of the Osage mission notes, the Osages eventually began to understand the meaning of salvation of the soul. Showing greater respect for the Black Robes, they more willingly offered their children for baptism and for further instruction. Also, the adults who accepted the faith produced Christians of good and even outstanding morals.[23]

After working with Native Americans for over two hundred years, the Jesuits came to know them fairly well. On one occasion the Canadian missionary, Father L. F. Nau, wrote to Father Bonn, his provincial: "The Iroquois and Hurons are more inclined to the practice of virtue than other nations . . . If there were no French in Canada, we would have as many saints in our mission as we now have Christians, but the bad example and solicitations of the French are a very great obstacle to the sanctification of our Iroquois."[24] Father Miege, even before his consecration as bishop, saw an even worse situation emerging for the Plains Indians. He wrote to his family: "You know that they are about to build a railroad which will cross the desert to the Pacific Ocean: this will be a 'bagatelle' of more than 1,500 leagues [4,500 miles]. This will perhaps be the end of these poor natives, who will be thus obliged to move northward for their hunting, and to wage continued war with the tribes whose lands they invade. At least it will result in continued association with the whites; and this is the worst evil that could possibly strike them, because of the liquor they sell them and the vices they teach them. . . . "[25]

With the Great Plains Indians, it was not only a matter of "fire water" being made available it was also a matter of the very presence of the white people themselves. The writings of the Jesuit Fathers echo the complaints of the Indians, who insisted that white men wrongfully enter Osage camps during hunting season, occupy their homes and fields, and refuse to move. From the *Historia Domus Missionis Osagianae (History of the Osage Mission)* we learn that the Fathers were finding it difficult to persuade their charges to submit patiently. Even when they did so they continued to burn with anger against the white settlers, thus making it impossible to fill their minds with higher thoughts.[26] It is surprising that the Fathers accomplished as much as they did. The *Litterae Annuae (Annual Letters)* shows that from July 1870 to July 1871, for example, there were 164 infant and 24 adult baptisms, 30 marriages, and 230 confirmations.[27]

The Jesuits were able to help the natives in other ways too. For example, when Bishop Miege first visited the Osages in late June 1851, he found them in dire need due to crop failures and back payments still owed to them by the government. Accordingly, the bishop wrote to the Commissioner of Indian Affairs, asking him to right the situation. The letter dated July 18, 1851, reads as follows:

> The undersigned Bishop of the Indian Territory begs to present the following memorial.
>
> Owing to a successive failure of crops, the Osage Mission has been, for the last two years, laboring under the effects of scarcity and comparative indigency hardly relieved by the efforts of the Director to procure at a great distance & at a great expense the very necessaries of life. The Government grant, which in ordinary circumstances would have sufficed, has not been found adequate.

The deficiency has been supplied by the Undersigned out of his private resources. He would then petition the Department for a special appropriation to meet the exigencies of the case, and if directed to name the amount, he would state a sum of 1,200 dollars—indulging the hope that abundant harvests henceforward will render such an appeal unnecessary.

The Undersigned begs also to call the attention of the Department of the petition presented last year by the Osages for the establishment of Catholic schools on the Verdigris to meet the wants of a numerous portion of their tribe settled on its banks. The Undersigned, should the prayer of the petitioners be granted, would beg respectfully to be informed, 1st what amount would be allotted for building and for farming outfit, 2nd, what sum would be appropriated for educational purposes. When many pupils are educated together, at the usual sum allowed for each by the Department, a proper economy enables the Directors to meet annual expenses—a result wholly unattainable when a limited appropriation admits of receiving but a small number.[28]

Ten years later, the bishop wrote from Leavenworth encouraging one of the Jesuits, visiting or about to visit Washington, D.C., to petition the government for "the amount due the two Missions." In particular he thought the government in all fairness should grant two points: one "to secure the allowance so far granted for every pupil" and another "to obtain the necessary funds to put up suitable buildings for school purposes."[29] Miege was, in time, to become a great champion of the Indians "in the name of the principles of equality and freedom of our Constitution." Shortly before Kansas was opened to white settlers, he wrote: "It makes me sick to think of the way these poor savages have been treated and will be to the end."[30] Writing to his brother in December 1852, he pointed out that the Osages not long ago possessed all the land lying within Missouri and Arkansas and extending indefinitely toward New Mexico. He added: "The government has been able to buy their best lands for practically nothing, and they are now relegated to the banks of the Neosho or Grant River, and the Verdigris, to go out into the interior of the plains three times a year to hunt buffalo or procure a few enemy scalps."[31] Father Paul Ponziglione wrote the following letter to a friend:

> If during a period of forty-nine years, the Osages, as a nation did not take up arms against the United States government; if they did not make a wholesale slaughter of trains and caravans while crossing the plains; if they did not ransack the country along the border of both the Missouri and Kansas; if, in a word, they did not turn hostile to the white people, this is due, in a great part to the influence of the Catholic Church exerted over them through her missionaries.[32]

To develop and maintain this kind of influence required considerable financial help. We should recall here that Miege, though a bishop, retained his status as a Jesuit. As long as he remained at Saint Mary's, the finances of the missions, as well as the spiritual and physical well-being of the Jesuits throughout the vicariate, were his concern. He took his commission quite seriously. In the spring of 1852, measles, scurvy, and typhoid played havoc among the Osages. When the bishop sent Father Bax a batch of vaccine, he almost got the mission literally burned to the ground. The Native Americans thought that the Black Robes were trying to kill them. Meanwhile, Father Bax, working day and night with the sick and the dying, himself became ill and was finally sent to Fort Scott to recover. When Bishop Miege stopped off at the fort on July 31, the Feast of Saint Ignatius, he found the good father on his death bed. In a report to Father General Roothaan the following month he declared:

> Our good and zealous Father Bax left us to receive in Paradise the recompense of his pains and fatigues, which so well filled the 5 years of his apostolate in the midst of the Indians. On August 5 an hour and a half after midnight Father Schoenmakers and I heard his last sigh at Fort Scott 40 miles from our Mission. The only sentiments I have been able to understand about him is the complete sacrifice of his life, which he offered to the good God for the conversion and salvation of his

beloved Osages. Would that the good God had been content with a dead member like myself. I prayed earnestly that he would take me instead of the best of my missionaries, but that was not heeded, and behold our poor Osages from whom we were beginning to expect something, again without a missionary who speaks their language, and who consequently can obtain their complete confidence.[33]

The bishop was also concerned about the death of Chief White Hair, who had been baptized, confirmed, and received his first communion the previous year. His willingness to listen to the advice of Father Bax, together with his influence over the Osages, had been a great help to the missionaries. As the bishop remarked to Roothaan, "What remains . . . is the courage of Father Schoenmakers, the goodwill of Father Ponziglione, and above all the hope that the good God, for whom it seems to me one works here, will aid his workers and have pity on our poor Natives."[34]

Bishop Miege followed Saint Ignatius's advice that one work as though everything depended on oneself but pray as though everything depended on God. We find him most watchful over the spiritual well-being of the Jesuits under his care. Thus, in July 1852, he wrote to Father Roothaan that the fathers and brothers at the Potawatomi mission were doing quite well and that "the spiritual exercises were performed regularly." Whenever the fathers had to take a trip or the brothers go off to buy provisions, he recommended that they make their meditation and examen of conscience. He admitted though that meditation in the midst of such distractions was not easy but that the good God would take account of their goodwill. Spiritual reading and exhortations were made punctually, while catechism (for the brothers) was taught every other week. Throughout his life Bishop Miege retained the greatest love and affection for his Jesuit brethren.[35]

Generally speaking, Bishop Miege's source of revenue for the missions was threefold: government subsidies, private contributions, and the mission farm. From 1838 to 1855, for example, the Indian Office supplied the Catholic Potawatomi with $43,837.52. Until 1855 every child educated at the mission was allotted $50.00 per year. This sum was not enough to support the mission, however. Further help came from generous persons in both Europe and America. The Lyons Association for the Propagation of the Faith was particularly helpful. Normally such benefactions came to Father De Smet since he was procurator for the mission, and he, in turn, would distribute them where needed.

Saint Mary's Mission Farm was a third source of revenue. In 1855 Father Duerinck reported:

> We have raised this season sixty acres oats, forty corn, six potatoes, the oats very heavy. . . . The corn and potatoes bid fair to yield a good crop. Our horned stock consists of two hundred and fifty head; say, eighty cows, fifteen yoke of oxen, forty two-year old steers—the balance is young cattle of our own raising. We derive no inconsiderable part of our support from our stock. There is also a good demand for corn, potatoes, oats, which the mission as well as the Indians can sell at fair prices.[36]

Much of the stock mentioned in the father's account seems to have originated in "the weak and disabled cattle left behind on the California trail by outgoing emigrants and convoys." Such emigrants were happy to get rid of newly born stock that could not have stood the rigors of the trail.

On one occasion, while he was a professor at Saint Xavier College in Cincinnati, Father Duerinck had met Cyrus McCormick, inventor of the reaper. As early as 1852 one of the McCormick mowing machines was used at Saint Mary's— probably for the first time in the grasslands—and it was the wonder of the countryside. People came from the surrounding area to see these horse-drawn machines. An 1853 model used at the mission cut "at least 500 tons of hay and oats . . . without any material break." In October 1854, McCormick asked Father Duerinck to sell his machines, an offer that was ultimately rejected.[37]

Heavy machinery, such as a McCormick mower, would probably have come up the Kaw by one of the steamboats that plied the river at high water. In 1864 the Kansas legislature declared the Kaw and its tributaries non-navigable and authorized the railroads to erect bridges over them. While it lasted such river traffic benefitted the mission.[38]

5

THE EUROPEAN INTERLUDE

It was not long before Bishop Miege began to realize that there was not much for him to do of an episcopal character in the Indian Territory. He had visited the Osage Mission and was living at Saint Mary's. Other foundations were needed, but he lacked both men and funds. Even financing the existing missions had its problems. What resources he did have came from the government, from charitable gifts, and from the mission farms. The first was helpful but inadequate, the second was impaired because of the strife in Europe at the time, and the third was still in its infancy.

There was one matter that seems to have been a source of embarrassment for the bishop. On October 30, 1851, Father General Roothaan wrote to Father William Murphy, provincial of the St. Louis vice province, informing him that: "The direction of the Mission in as far as it is a mission, belongs to [the bishop] and for this he depends only on Propaganda. There is nothing then to do but to get along with one another in harmony."[1] This situation was maintained until the bishop left Saint Mary's for Leavenworth, when local superiors were placed in full charge of the missions. Fortunately, Bishop Miege was a humble man, prudent in his dealings with the Jesuit superiors, such as Father Duerinck, superior of the Potawatomi Mission, and with whom he had cordial relations.

Meanwhile, the bishop continued to further the spiritual welfare of the communities under his care. We get some idea of his character in a letter he wrote to Father Roothaan in July 1852.[2] In addition to studying the Indian languages, he spent time teaching catechism to the children. He also gave religious instruction to the Jesuit brothers and to the Sisters of the Sacred Heart who conducted the school for girls at Saint Mary's. We know, too, that on one occasion in 1852 he hastened to the banks of the Missouri River with a physician to offer relief to a band of cholera-stricken non-Christian Potawatomi Indians on their way from Michigan to Kansas. More than once, the bishop had trouble convincing the Indians that inoculation would help them rather than cause serious illness or even death.

Bishop Miege's fairly peaceful existence was to end abruptly in 1853. In March of that year the Provincial Congregation of the St. Louis vice province acted in an unusual manner. They elected John Baptist to represent them as a delegate to the Twenty-second General Congregation of the Society to be held in Rome. The bishop's reaction to the election is nicely captured in a letter he wrote to the Father General:

My Very Reverend Father,

I have just received a letter from Rev. Father Murphy in which as much as he can, as he says, he asks me to come to St. Louis as soon as possible, so that I can leave for Rome on the 15th of April in the capacity of procurator of the Vice-Province at the General Congregation which is set to open on June 21.

St. Louis! Rome! Procurator! General Congregation!!!! What a lot of great things for my grandeur. I will go to St. Louis, my very Reverend Father, and there I will say that it is an affront to the Vice Province to have it represented by a poor shameless old vicar almost a stranger to the affairs of those who are sending him, having no knowledge of the Institute and none of the qualifications required by the Company for such a mission.

If after having spoken so clearly, openly, with the firm wish of being understood, they want me to make the journey, I will make it. . . . [Copy unclear here]

It is certain that if I go to Rome and the Good God puts in my tongue the petitions he has sometimes put into my head, Your Reverence will be touched. You will go with me to the Holy Father and meanwhile you will pray as you know how. I will speak. I will say that for two years His Holiness has been mistaken in his choice of the Vicar and perhaps also in the erection of the Vicariate, and that it is surely time to have pity on the one if he does not wish to suppress the other. I will prove that it is necessary, and with the help of the good God and your prayers, my very Reverend Father, I will win.[3]

In St. Louis, Bishop Miege was urged to accept the appointment as delegate, and so in April 1853, accompanied by Father De Smet, he set out for Europe.[4] On arrival overseas he went first to Rome where he made his *ad limina* visit to Pope Pius IX. Garin tells us that the pope remembered the young Savoyard Jesuit. Miege's commanding presence had impressed the pontiff during a visit to the Roman College in 1847. He received the missionary bishop with great kindness and encouragement. Did this most gracious reception deter Miege from presenting his resignation? We do not know. If indeed he did present his request, nothing came of it.

After the work of the Congregation, which elected Peter Beckx as Father General, was completed, Bishop Miege went to Turin. There he was given a number of church supplies and several sacred vessels. Here, and elsewhere, he was not very successful in procuring funds for his mission. Nor, in the course of his European visit, was he able to obtain very many recruits. He did, however, acquire an oil painting of the Immaculate Virgin, which may still be seen in the present parish church at Saint Mary's, Kansas.

Toward the end of July, John Baptist arrived at Chevron, France, where he took a few weeks of rest in the company of friends and relatives. One can imagine the joy, particularly of his dear brother Urban who had not seen him for so long a time. It seems that John Baptist's fellow countrymen and women came to have considerable regard for the "little rascal" who had so distinguished himself in the American missions. We may be sure that his letters to Urban had been read and talked about far and wide. Garin tells us that the Curé of

Left to right: L. Miege, Bishop Miege, Canon
Alliaudi, and Curé Marjolet. Reprinted from Joseph
Garin, *Les Évêques et Prêtres de Chevron*
(Albertville, France: Libraire M. Papet, 1936).

Chevron, the Abbé Marjolet, took advantage of Miege's popu-
larity by organizing an imposing ceremony at which the
bishop pontificated, assisted by a large number of priests
and laity.[5]

From what Garin tells us, the bishop's friends and relatives
were delighted to listen to his stories of the missions. They
were particularly interested in hearing about Indian customs,
such as their manner of eating at celebrations—large quanti-
ties of buffalo meat and fowl would be eaten with fingers off
a common dish. The bishop mentioned how he had a very
difficult time eating a special dish of meat that was first masti-
cated by the women and then passed around. When the dish
came to him, he would put a cigar or sprinkle some tobacco
on it and then hand it to his neighbor, who would then eat a
double portion. We gather that the good bishop ate his share
as time went on.[6]

Bishop Miege left Chevron in September to continue his
efforts to secure help for his missions in the form of gifts and
labor. At Paris, on November 18, he joined Father De Smet
and his recruits. There is a bit of confusion as to the exact
number of these prospective missionaries. De Smet refers to
the eight young men who accompanied him, but in the same
letter he mentions his leaving his "thirteen companions for an
hour" to search for some misplaced boxes.[7] On the other
hand, Garin states that on November 22 Bishop Miege started
again from Havre for the New World, taking with him fifteen

missionaries who had consented to join him in his work of evangelization.[8] Bishop Miege himself tells us that, when the party reached Havre on November 21, it included "some Belgians, some Hollanders, one German, one Frenchman, one Swiss, two Piedmontese, and one Roman, fifteen in all."[9]

Father De Smet had his problems. When time came to board the ship, his companions were nowhere to be found. For six hours, with the help of some eight or ten volunteers, he combed the streets and wharves of Havre. A gendarme finally informed him that his group was already aboard ship. Thinking they were late, they had hired two small boats to take them to the steamer. When Father De Smet finally boarded he found the ship swarming with gendarmes, who were carefully examining all passports. De Smet explains:

> My travelling companions were all provided, except one, who had joined me in Paris, with the consent of his parents. I was not without anxiety in his regard; but our young deserter, M.M***, disguised as a cabin-boy, played his part perfectly; he held the lantern to aid the police-officers in a manner to do honor to the most skillful cabin-boy, during their whole visit to the saloons and cabins. All the passengers passed in review, all the passports were minutely criticized; but the agents paid no attention to the handsome lantern-bearer, who always remained close by them, and thus quietly escaped their scrutiny. My anxiety, however, did not subside until I saw the gentlemen leave our decks.[10]

The ship belonging to the bishop's sailing party was the *Humboldt*, considered to be one of the most beautiful of American steamers. Anchor was raised at nightfall on November 22 and, after a brief stop for passenger and mail pick-up and delivery at Cahos on the Isle of Wight, the ship entered the ocean the evening of the twenty-third. According to Miege, "it received us in a bad humor and it treated us accordingly until the end." Bishop Miege's account of the voyage is essentially the same as Father De Smet's; however, we prefer to give the latter's fascinating account since it tells us much of the hazards of ocean travel in the midnineteenth century. De Smet writes:

For fourteen days the *Humboldt* combated against a stormy sea and violent west wind; Neptune received this time a double tribute from those who were so bold as to hazard crossing his domain in this season of the year. The great sufferer was Bishop Miege, who kept his bed constantly. The next was young Fortune Hegel, of Brussels, who has too weak a stomach ever to make a good sailor; he supported this misery with great forti- tude, never regretting that he had left his quiet home for some years. All the others escaped tolerably; as to myself, I felt almost no inconvenience from sea-sickness during the whole voyage. To the violent storms of wind we must add several other disagreeable circumstances— the steam-engine got out of order several times, and the boilers threatened to blow us in the air; the coal was of a bad quality, and that, even, began to become scarce on the twelfth day of our voyage. We were obliged to devi- ate from our ordinary route, to get a supply of coal at Halifax, a seaport of Nova Scotia. This neglect on the part of the company was extremely fatal in its conse- quences.

In the forenoon of the 6th of December, about five leagues from port, a fisherman presented himself on board as a pilot, and declared to the captain, who demanded his certificates, "that his papers were either in his boat, or at his own house." The captain relied upon his word, and entrusted him with the management of the ship. Against the expressed opinion of the officers, the false pilot changed the boat's direction, and notwith- standing their reiterated remonstrances, he persisted in his obstinacy. An hour and a half afterwards, the *Humboldt* struck on the dangerous rocks called "The Sisters," in the neighborhood of Devil's Island. It was half-past six in the morning—the greater number of the passengers were still in their berths. The shock was ter- rific; I was walking on the deck at the moment. Discovering directly great pieces of wood floating on the surface of the water, I hastened to warn all my compan- ions of their danger, for they were also still in their beds. Young Hegel having been entrusted to me by his father, I took him by my side as long as the danger lasted, and kept a rope in my hand for the purpose of lowering him into the first life-boat that should be launched. All had been startled from sleep. Fear had palsied every heart; and while the water was pouring into the vessel by torrents, fire broke out. It was got under but by great exertion, through the presence of mind and manly energy of the first engineer; after great efforts, they succeeded in extinguishing it. As if all things conspired to our destruction, a fog arose, so thick that we could not see thirty paces from the vessel. The whole power of the steam-engine was exerted in an attempt to gain the shore, six miles distant. The boat soon inclined to the larboard side, where she had sprung a leak, and began to go down. Every arm set to work to aid in launching the small-boats. Had not the captain exhibited great presence of mind and an extraordinary firmness, there would have been much tumult and disorder. There was a rush to get in first, but happily we were not obliged to resort to this means of saving ourselves. While the greater number believed that all was lost, and I among the rest, the ship touched again, in a few fathoms of water, and rested on a rock. We were saved!

Immediately after the shipwreck, the fog rose, and we then discovered, for the first time and to our joyful surprise, that the shore was only one hundred feet from us. The sea was calm, the wind lowered, and the sun rose majestically. It was the announcement of a return of fine weather, which left us at Havre de Grâce, and now accompanied us until we reached Missouri. We had the good fortune and the time to save all our trunks, traveling bags, and boxes. The loss of the ship and cargo was estimated at $600,000.[11]

In the matter of an hour or two a steamboat came out to take the passengers to Halifax, then a city of some twenty-five thousand souls. On December 8, the bishop's party boarded the *Niagara*, of the Liverpool and Boston line. The trip to Boston was uneventful with the exception of a man who openly declared himself to be an enemy of all existing creeds, especially the pope and the Jesuits. On leaving Liverpool he had announced publicly that he would kill the first Jesuit he met on American soil. Fortunately for the bishop and his companions, the captain had relieved the man of his gun, his pistols, and his daggers. Father De Smet noted that he was "but a fanatic more for these States, which have already unfortunately received thousands from all the various countries of Europe. These creatures begin to agitate, to harangue, to seek to change the Constitution, and make the United States a land of proscription, especially against the Catholics."[12]

Bishop Miege and his companions rested for a few days in Boston, which with its population of 150,000 inhabitants had earned the nickname of "Athens of the West." They then traveled by train via Buffalo, Cleveland, and Columbus to Cincinnati, and by boat down the Ohio and up the Mississippi River to St. Louis. Travel of this kind was quite dangerous in the midnineteenth century. As late as 1890, railroad accidents in the United States caused ten thousand deaths and eighty thousand serious injuries. Primitive technology was partly at fault, but apparently much of the blame was to be laid at the feet of management. As George T. Strong put it: "We shall never travel safely till some pious, wealthy, and much beloved railroad director has been hanged for murder. . . ."[13] Father De Smet tells of the "risk" the party was taking during its fifty-two hour, 750-mile trip to Cincinnati. He wrote:

> Be not astonished at the word *"risk,"* for accidents on all the routes are of frequent occurrence, and often frightful. Today, it may be that a bridge has been left open——a hairbrained or intoxicated engineer pays no attention, and locomotive and cars are precipitated into the water; tomorrow two trains will meet in collision, dashing into each other with all the velocity that steam can create. In a word there are all kinds of accidents. When they occur, a list is given of the killed and disabled, which is often a very considerable one, curious inquiries are made, and some days after there is no further mention of the affair.[14]

River travel in the mid-1800s was equally risky. Upstream travel in the spring, when the current was swift, put a great strain on the boilers. "[S]ubject to no rigorous design or maintenance codes," according to Otto L. Bettman, these boilers "were as lethal as bombs, and the danger to life was magnified by the malfunction of on-board safety equipment, or indeed its absence." Even the old Mississippi riverboats, outwardly magnificent, were not what they seemed to be. Rather, they were "crowded to capacity, bustling with gambling sharks and ruffians and pervaded by the compound aroma of food, cattle excrement, and decaying straw. And explosions, fires, and collisions were the order of the day."[15] During the winter months the rivers were low, full of sawyers, sand banks, and floating ice. It is not surprising then that the boat on which the Jesuits traveled ran aground three times while ascending the Mississippi. They were more fortunate than the five Lazarists, fellow travelers on the *Humboldt,* who arrived in St. Louis some days earlier. After suffering a shipwreck on the Mississippi they had to wade ashore in water up to their necks. No wonder Bishop Miege preferred not to travel during the winter months for the rest of his life.

6

THE COMING OF THE WHITE SETTLERS

After a brief delay at St. Louis due to the frozen condition of the Mississippi River—and, one could speculate, the Missouri—Bishop Miege finally arrived at Saint Mary's in March 1854, where he was given a warm reception by his flock. They marveled at the wondrous things he brought back with him—chalices, ostensoria, vestments, the painting of the Immaculate Conception, and rosary beads blessed by the pope. They were particularly amazed with the organ, which, as Father Gailland once observed, porduced the most agreeable music with the slightest touch of the fingers.

In May, two months after the prelate arrived back in his vicariate, an event occurred that brought chaos to the hitherto peaceful valley of the Kaw, indeed to all of Kansas. On May 30, 1854, President Franklin Pierce signed the Kansas-Nebraska Act, a piece of legislation that divided the former Indian Territory, except for the present state of Oklahoma, into the territories of Kansas and Nebraska. Whereas slavery had been prohibited in the Indian Territory, now by a process called *popular sovereignty* the two territories, upon achieving statehood status, would be either free or slave, depending on their constitutions. The Act further stipulated that nothing contained in it should be "construed to impair the rights of persons or property now pertaining to the Indians in said

Territory. . . ." (Section 1) Earlier, on March 3, 1853, Congress had authorized the president to negotiate with the Indians west of the Iowa–Missouri line in order to secure cession of their lands for fifty thousand dollars.

Before leaving for Europe, Bishop Miege had written from St. Louis to the vicar general in Rome informing him of what was happening. In the letter, dated April 15, 1853, he declared that "this treaty will embrace all the tribes between the 36th and the 43rd degree of latitude, and will have as its object to buy from the Natives all their lands, except the portion that the government would grant to those who wished to live peacefully among the Whites. Your Reverence can easily see that this is the sentence of death for the larger part of our poor diocesans, a sentence nevertheless that was feared for a long time and which, as a consequence, astonishes nobody. What will become of the two established missions?"[1]

Father De Smet had the answer. Somewhat bitterly, he wrote: "It is not difficult to descry from afar that grand event which must engulf in one common wreck all the Indian tribes. The storm which has just burst forth over their heads was long preparing; it could not escape the observing eye. We saw the American Republic soaring, with the rapidity of the eagle's flight, toward the plenitude of her power. Every year she adds new countries to her limits. . . . Her object is obtained. All bend to her sceptre; all Indian nationality is at her feet."[2] On the other hand, Father Duerinck tended to welcome the Act of 1854 as introducing "salutary laws and the fear of punishment," something that would restrain evil-minded persons who had already entered Kansas along the California–Oregon and Santa Fe trails. Unfortunately, it would take several years before these "salutary laws" took effect in Kansas. The story of political strife there and how it affected Bishop Miege will be told presently.

Meanwhile, the good vicar was faced with a real problem. As much as he regretted the fact, he saw that the days of Indian independence were numbered and that whites would soon be pouring into the newly opened territories. As bishop he was responsible for the latter as well as for the former. Amid such changing conditions, Saint Mary's Mission was no longer satisfactory as headquarters for the vicariate. The sudden growth of Kansas was nothing short of amazing. In mid-

1854 the territory consisted of three government forts, a half-dozen missions, and a few stopping-off places along the Santa Fe Trail. Four years later, a listing of towns included Wyandotte, Delaware, Douglas, Maryville, Iola, Atchison, Fort Scott, Pawnee, Lecompton, Neosho, Richmond, Lawrence, Doniphan, Paola, Indianola, Easton, and Leavenworth.[3] Even Saint Mary's, situated as it was on the California–Oregon Trail, began to take on the aspects of a town.

In the midst of all this turmoil Bishop Miege decided to move his residence. From the beginning he seems to have chosen Leavenworth, then the most promising of the new settlements, as his new location. Writing to Urban he mentioned that the governor and his deputies, hearing of his decision to move while on a visit to Saint Mary's, strongly urged him to locate in the same place that they would chose for a capital. "But," he added, "I am afraid to listen to them. Their goodwill goes as far as their private interest and there they stop." He then told Urban how, at a spot below Fort Leavenworth, they were actually building a nice town that had the same name as the fort. "It is one of the loveliest locations on the Missouri," he wrote.[4] A "nice location" and offer of money no doubt played no small part in affirming his decision to move to Leavenworth. He left Saint Mary's on August 9, 1855, accompanied by Brother Francis Roig, S.J. At that point, he entrusted the missions to the care of his Jesuit brethren, and he devoted most of his attention to the pioneers who were flooding into his vicariate.

Before departing for Leavenworth, Bishop Miege made a very important trip into the Nebraska Territory, then still a part of his vicariate. In mid-March he set out with his mules and an old spring wagon that had once been used to deliver milk in the streets of St. Louis. The wagon was a gift from Father De Smet—he had originally used it in his missionary work. According to the bishop, "the mules were rich in years, as well as in skin and bones."[5]

On his way north the bishop crossed over into Missouri and then, after many days of camping and traveling, made his way roughly to Council Bluffs, Iowa, where he crossed the river to Omaha. In spite of the fine weather, good grass for the mules, and lots of game, it was not an easy trip. On one occasion, a mule lost its footing while trotting down a steep slope, fell down, broke the bishop's harness, and caused the "carriage" to pile up on him. Fortunately, the bishop escaped and the mule was not injured. After an hour's work he resumed the journey. When the bishop arrived at the ferry "the wind was so strong that the little steam ferry refused to move."[6] In a hurry to continue his journey, he accepted an invitation to cross over in a canoe. It did not take long for the little skiff to fill with water, but still the bishop retained his good humor, remarking that he "might become the largest fish in the Missouri River."[7] Though wet and covered with mud he reached the west bank unharmed.

The bishop tells us that he made his way to the Douglas House in Omaha where he met Mrs. Cuming, wife of the governor, who told him where he might find his excellency. The governor informed him that two lots had been reserved for a Catholic church and that more could be secured if necessary. Bishop Miege was delighted with the site at Omaha and promised the governor to send a priest there as soon as possible. When he returned in the spring of 1857, he found that a small brick church had been built. On this occasion he made the acquaintance of "the excellent Creighton family" and promised to do what he could to obtain a resident vicar apostolic for Nebraska.[8]

On arriving back at Saint Mary's, Bishop Miege gave an account of his trip to Father General Beckx. Although the letter is somewhat lengthy, we cite it here since it gives valuable information on the condition of the vicariate as well the situation in Kansas at the time:

My Very Reverend Father:

Here I am just back from a long journey in Nebraska made to get some idea, more or less exact, of the Catholic population of this new Territory. I found Catholics just about everywhere, but not in sufficiently large numbers to provide for the support of a resident priest in their midst. As the population goes on growing daily, I have accepted or bought lots in the principal little towns which have been begun since last Autumn. These towns in Nebraska are Omaha City, Bellevue, Platteville, Karney City, Nebraska City. I gave $500 (piastres) for a church in Omaha City, where there is already a good number of Catholics, and I paid $200 for 8 lots in Karney City. In other places they liberally donated the necessary land for church and schools.

The Tribe of the Omahas, which last year occupied the land on which these towns are being built, has kept for itself, some 50 miles further in the interior, a rich section of land where they say they want to have schools run by the black-robes. . . . The funds appropriated for their schools are $1,400 a year whether they have more pupils or less. I have written to Reverend Father Murphy begging him to accept this offer for principally two reasons: 1. the school having a good yearly income will give little temporal trouble, 2. the Fathers being only 50 miles from the principal places where the whites are settling will easily be able to visit them and give them basic instruction. Many Catholics are rushing to the two new territories and I do not have a priest to give them. I have written to Ireland, to France, and to Savoy for help but still no answer. If the Society at least does not come to my help, I see no other way than to take a mule and my gun and hide myself in some crevice of the Rocky Mountains, where I will no longer be able to hear about the needs and the miseries of Kansas and Nebraska. I have voyaged, or rather run by mule steamer, one easily understands, almost without interruption since mid-March to the end of June, visiting a good part of the two territories. Troubles, fatigue, embarrassments are never wanting in this manner of travel, but this would assuredly be nothing if one's heart did not constantly overflow with pain and chagrin because of the isolation and woes of so many poor souls to whom the Vicar Apostolic by himself alone cannot afford relief.

The Vice-Province of Missouri, to my mind, has not done quite all it might have for many years, but it is poor in subjects, and it will be impossible to help me according to my needs. May I be permitted, My Very Reverend Father, to ask you if some of our flourishing European Provinces could not supply Kansas and Nebraska with a few missionaries for the salvation of the German and Irish people arriving among us? Such a proposition should not be made to reverend Father Ponza, since he

seems to be determined to take from me Father Ponziglione who has already been with the Osages for 4
years; I have asked Reverend Father Murphy to answer
him that if I am so unfortunate as not to be able to
obtain either Fathers or Secular priests, I shall at least be
able to hold the 5 I have to work along the 14 degrees of
latitude without mentioning the longitude. He can cry,
make an uproar, threaten, do and say all he pleases. I am
more than determined not to listen either with the right
ear or the left. And I have with all that the firm hope that
your Paternity will have the great kindness to forgive me
this rare sort of whim, which can only be pardoned in a
poor Vicar Apostolic who permits himself to engage in it.

The excitement caused in the Territory of Kansas by
the slavery question draws the attention of the United
States. The two parties dispute over it and each is sending its contingent of immigrants. All that has been sold
by the Indians has long since been occupied. All our
plains and woodlands are now taken up by farms and
newborn towns. The main ones are Leavenworth, Delaware, Atchison, Doniphan on the Missouri, Laurence, [sic]
Francklin, Lecompton, Benicia, Topeka, Fremont,
Whitfield, Indianola, St. George, Manhatan, Pawnee,
Reeder, Montgomery, on the Kansas River, Awsakee,
Osawatomie, Iola, Nemaha, Jacksonville, Fort Scott on
different small rivers of the Territory. At Doniphan they
are building a church for which I gave $300 (ecus), at
Pawnee I paid $150 for some lots, and given a contract
for a small house and a chapel of stone which will cost
$1,300. At Leavenworth which is, and will be, the best
town in the whole territory I have bought 23 lots for
which I paid $1,675. I have also bought 40 acres a mile
from town for $255. A house is being erected, although
built of wood it will cost me $1,800; a wooden chapel
which I am going to construct there as soon as the house
is completed will come to $800 plus a stable for $300. As
Your Paternity sees, it is a lot of money for a town which
numbers but 900 inhabitants, and 6 months existence.
There will remain further embarrassments to obtain titles
for the lots and the claims bought, since the whole finds
itself on prohibited land, that is, land on which the

Government has forbidden the Whites to settle. Four or five thousand people have settled on it. The Government has frequently complained, but has taken no effective means to drive them away. This has encouraged others, and I among them following the advice of the Fathers of the Mission and of many well informed persons, who have done the same as I. We will probably be cleared by the payment of a little additional amount which will satisfy the Government and leave us the advantages of the first purchase. I will give Your Paternity an account of the final result . . . .

My expenses this year will be at least $8,000 (ecus), and truly I am frightened over the coming year. Everything is still to be done, to be created so to speak, and if, by the strictest economy of four years, I had not succeeded in amassing a few thousand ecus, which now keep me from being embarrassed, the post would not be tenable by any means. . . . I hope that the allowance for last year, of which I have thus far heard nothing, will enable me to provide for the needs of the Vicariate. I am not at all preaching for myself in speaking in this manner. I am an ox or a horse, which is simply breaking ground, nothing more. I want to try to do well so that my successor has better days and more time to work for the salvation of souls.[9]

Bishop Miege was not long in fulfilling his promise to his friends in Nebraska to try to obtain a vicar for them. At the meeting of the First Provincial Council of St. Louis, presided over by Archbishop Peter Kenrick, from October 7 to 14, 1855, he made known his many problems. There was the ever-increasing flow of people coming into the area, for example, many of whom were Catholics. It was impossible to reach them with travel conditions, such as they were, through a land that lacked roads and bridges. Further, it made sense to create a Vicariate of Nebraska separate from that of Kansas. The bishops of the province, coming from such widely distant places as Dubuque, Nashville, Milwaukee, and Santa Fe, unanimously agreed with their colleague from the Indian Territory. They suggested to Rome that Nebraska be turned into a separate vicariate with Father De Smet as vicar and that

Bishop Miege be made ordinary of the newly established diocese of Kansas.[10]

It was not until February 17, 1857, that Cardinal Barnabo,
Prefect of the Propaganda, announced that Pius IX had
approved the proposed division. The new Vicariate of
Nebraska stretched from the fortieth parallel in the south to
the Canadian border in the north and from the Missouri River
in the east to the Rocky Mountains in the west. Meanwhile,
until a vicar could be appointed in 1859, Bishop Miege continued to care for the spiritual needs of this vast territory as
well as of his own beloved Kansas. In 1856 he found a good
recruit in Father John Cavanagh, fresh from Ireland, and sent
him to Omaha to care for Nebraska City. For the next several
months Father Cavanagh and Father Jeremiah Tracy were the
only Catholic priests in a "parish" scattered over 353,558
square miles. Further help was forthcoming in 1857 when
Father Augustine Wirth, O.S.B., began his work in southeast-
ern Nebraska. In the course of his visit in 1855, Bishop Miege
paid $3.00 for eight lots of land in Nebraska City. It was a
good investment indeed. Five years later, in 1860, Father
Philip Vogt, O.S.B., became the first pastor of what is now the
oldest church in Nebraska. Saint Benedict's Church was completed in 1861 and dedicated by Bishop James O'Gorman.
The cost of the structure, with its tower, was $4,000. The
bricks seem to have been made from local clay by parishioners. The original bell that graced the tower was salvaged
from the wreck of the river boat *Kansas*, which ran aground
in the vicinity of Sonora, Missouri. In 1865 work began on an
addition to the church. Eventually it would become the first
Catholic school in the area. This is only one of the many pio-
neering efforts for which Bishop Miege was responsible.

Some years later Father Ponziglione described very nicely
the growth process of the Catholic Church in Kansas. He
mentioned how, with the opening of Kansas in 1854 and the
coming of many Catholics to eastern Kansas, it became the
duty of the Jesuits to visit them occasionally. Gradually, new
mission stations were opened until every county had its own.
At the close of the Civil War, when the Osages ceded all their
reservations west of the Verdigris River to the government,
even newer fields opened for missionary labors. As soon as a
station could afford a church, it was built and a new congre-

gation was started. One after another such stations were turned over to Bishop Miege, who then placed them under the care of diocesan priests. Father Ponziglione adds: "So, through our missions, the Catholic religon has been established in twenty-seven counties. . . . Ours has been the work of pioneers, a hard and rough work, but we hope not the less meritorious before God . . . For nearly twenty-five years we have never had more than three priests residing at this Mission. . . . As for the Indians formerly living on their reservations within the boundaries of this State, they are all gone . . . all now moved into the Indian Territory south of us. . . . "[11]

Writing a few years earlier to Father Thomas O'Neil, provincial of the vice province of Missouri, Father Ponziglione gives us some idea of how pastors were placed in the new stations. Of two priests sent out by Bishop Miege in 1871, one was placed at Baxter Springs and charged with the care of Labette, Cherokee, and Crawford counties and a small part of the adjacent Indian Territory. The other was stationed at Cottonwood Falls. From there all the stations established on the Atchison, Topeka, and Santa Fe Railroad from Emporia in Lyon County to Wichita in Sedgewick County were under his jurisdiction. Well indeed could the good Father conclude: *"Messis quidem multa, operarii autem pauci,* the harvest is great, but the laborers are few."[12]

7

THE MOVE TO LEAVENWORTH

On August 9, 1855, Bishop Miege terminated his stay at Saint Mary's Mission. Packing his belongings on his "mule steamer" he set out for Leavenworth, accompanied by Brother Francis Roig. There, on August 15, he formally established his Cathedral Parish of the Immaculate Conception. Mass was celebrated on Shawnee Street in a one-story frame house owned by Andrew Quinn. A bureau served as an altar. Present was the entire Catholic population of Leavenworth, a total of nine families. Bishop Miege was not the first to say Mass in the Leavenworth area. Jesuits had come from the missions to celebrate Mass at the fort as early as 1836. Moreover, beginning in October 1854, Father William Fisch of Weston, Missouri, said Mass several times in the Quinn home before the bishop's arrival in Leavenworth.[1]

There was never a question in the bishop's mind regarding the name of the Cathedral Parish. Writing to his brother Urban in December 1854, he stated that the first church he built would be dedicated to the Immaculate Conception of the Most Blessed Virgin. He would dedicate, in a very special manner, himself and all his flock "to this truly good and loving mother." He further encouraged Urban to honor the Virgin in the same way and said that, in the future, he would "ask everything of the Blessed Virgin Mary through her

Early Leavenworth, Kansas. Source unknown.

Immaculate Conception."[2] It is not surprising that the bishop should have established the Sodality of the Immaculate Conception for men shortly after arriving in Leavenworth. Although he had difficulty finding the bare quorum of 7 members in 1855, five years later membership had risen to 128.[3]

Judging from his letter to Urban, John Baptist was planning to build a brick residence of seven or eight rooms. Not including the furniture, the cost would have amounted to some seventeen or eighteen thousand francs. He estimated that the church, if built with bricks, with a flat ceiling instead of a vault and maintaining a length of 125 feet, would cost forty-five thousand francs. Bewailing the expense of building anything in Kansas, he added: "So I am going to find myself in debt if the good God does not come to my help. I am counting on it." As it turned out, the house, built in 1855, was an unpretentious one-story affair that was given to the Sisters of Charity a few years later. The "cathedral" came to be a small frame structure, fifteen-by-twenty feet in size, built on the highest hill in town at the southwest corner of Kickapoo and Fifth streets. The cost, if we include a stable, came to about $1,100.[4] The following spring, in 1856, the church was enlarged. That same fall, with a congregation of six hundred souls, a third church had to be built. The first church worthy of the name "cathedral" was erected at Fifth and Kickapoo streets in 1859. By this time it was estimated that there were two thousand parishioners in the new town.[5] The influx of whites from Ireland, Germany, and the eastern United States was truly remarkable.

Upper: First residence of the bishop, circa 1851. Two years later, Bishop Miege constructed another two-story frame residence. *Lower:* First Cathedral of the Immaculate Conception, 1859. Fifth and Kickapoo streets, Leavenworth, Kansas. Reprinted from William J. McEvoy, *The "Old Cathedral" Parish 1855–1877* (Leavenworth, Kans.: Privately published, 1976?).

Kansas did not always welcome these newcomers too kindly. On the night of January 22, 1855, a terrible storm struck the territory. High winds drove snow everywhere. The bishop himself had a foot of it in his room and equally as much in the church. The poor immigrants who had just arrived had no time to prepare suitable dwellings and, thus, suffered terribly. One entire family—father, mother, and three children—were found frozen to death in their miserable hovel. Others experienced severe frostbite on their face and hands. One of the bishop's neighbors had fifteen cows freeze to death in the course of a night. "You see that all is not rosy in the land of freedom and abundance," the bishop remarked.[6] In August, he wrote to his brother: "We are surrounded on all sides by cholera; since spring it has caused great havoc principally on the Missouri and especially in Leavenworth. We are hoping that with September the plague will stop. All I ask of the good God is that he spare the six priests who constitute my entire resident clergy."[7]

The first official rector of the new cathedral was Reverend Theodore Heimann, who had been associated with the Jesuits at the Osage Mission. Father Heimann, who was also the first vicar general in Kansas, assumed his new duties in October 1855. The following fall another fine priest, Father James H. Defouri, came to Leavenworth. Like the bishop, he was a native of Savoy. He remained at the cathedral until the spring of 1862 when he moved to Topeka to become the first pastor of the Church of the Assumption. While at Topeka he established a seminary, and although it did not last long due to a lack of funds, no less than sixteen of its students were later ordained. Father Defouri seems to have been quite a scholar. Later, when he was made rector at the Leavenworth Cathedral, he gave special lessons in the classics. In his class were five boys from the parish; of these, four were later ordained.[8] The first priest to be ordained in Kansas by Bishop Miege was Casimir Seitz, a Benedictine deacon. The ordination took place in the humble little cathedral on the second Sunday after Easter in 1857.[9]

The arrival of several religious orders gave Bishop Miege every reason to be encouraged in his work of spreading the faith in Kansas. The Benedictines began their long fruitful mission in the person of Father Henry Lemke, O.S.B., who arrived at Lecompton, Kansas, around Christmas 1855. The following spring he made his way to Leavenworth and began to assist at the cathedral. Shortly thereafter he was sent to establish a church at Doniphan. At the time Father Henry was sixty years old. He was an interesting old warrior for Christ. A soldier in his youth, he later studied for the Lutheran ministry at the University of Rostock in northern Germany. He was granted his license to preach in 1820. Three years later, he converted to Catholicism. Soon after his confirmation he began his study of Catholic theology. He was ordained to the priesthood in 1826. Dissatisfied with the way his priestly life was tending, he decided to go to America and, with the blessing of his bishop, he arrived in Philadelphia in 1834. His life as a diocesan priest had its share of difficulties and so it was that, in 1852, he decided to become a Benedictine. After a year's novitiate he pronounced his vows in February 1853. His life as a Benedictine had its problems, too. An older man accustomed to independence, he found it difficult to serve under younger men. Moreover, he had his own ideas of what the vow of poverty was all about. He also seemed to have a bit of the Friar Tuck in his makeup. When his prior refused permission for him to go on a "begging" trip, he went anyway, traveling first to Westport, Missouri, and later to Leavenworth. There he fell under the influence of Bishop Miege whom he soon came to admire. Nobody was happier than the bishop when he heard that Father Henry had made his peace with Archabbot Boniface Wimmer back East.[10]

Father Henry lived in dire poverty in Doniphan on a large plot of land measuring 308 feet by 264 feet along Front Street. He began building a combination church and residence, but it was not completed before winter set in. Meanwhile, a fourteen-by-sixteen-foot shanty served as his residence. He notified Abbot Wimmer: "Nearby lives a family where I can wash, bake bread, and get milk and water. Mornings and evenings I make a little soup and tea or coffee. At noon I go to the local hotel so that I will have at least one good meal a day. I sleep on a straw sack which lies on a few boards nailed together."[11] Father Henry first said Mass for his three-family congregation in a room in the Doniphan House. His next church was a frame hut originally meant to be a carpenter shop. Affluent at age thirty-eight with a large congregation, at sixty he was practically destitute. When the cold became unbearable, he moved from his rented shanty to a lawyer's office, where a stove kept him warm. He had a bed there but soon gave this up to a young man dying of syphilis and returned to his straw pallet.[12] That winter he was called on more than once to minister to a dying soul out on the prairie. He had no horse and had on occasion to walk fifteen miles and more through snow and ice. Still, in the midst of all this, he seems to have been really happy for the first time in his life. Father Peter Beckman writes of him: "Father Henry was a restless and a cantankerous man. . . . Nevertheless, God managed to make use of him. He accepted real hardship in his zeal for souls, and the charity he demonstrated in giving his bed to a dying syphilitic speaks for itself . . . he is indelibly a part of . . . the beginning of St. Benedict's [Atchison, Kansas]."[13]

When Father Henry returned East in 1857 his place was taken at Doniphan by Father Augustine Wirth and the newly ordained Father Casimir Seitz. It was Father Wirth who, in 1858, moved to Atchison to establish the Benedictine monastery. By this time there were some forty Catholic families in Atchison. In August, Prior Augustine began building the first church, a small fifty by twenty-five-foot frame structure that stood on the site of the present Benedictine church.

In May 1864, Fathers Cyril Knoll and Xavier Huber, two members of the Carmelite Priory of Straubing, Germany, arrived in the United States. Their original intention was to establish a house of the order in Louisville, Kentucky. When that did not materialize, Bishop Miege invited them to Kansas. Arriving in Leavenworth on October 7, 1864, they were put in charge of Saint Joseph Church, which, according to the previous pastor, Father A. Kuhls, had six to seven hundred parishioners. Most were German-speaking. Father Knoll was surprised at what he saw in the territory of Kansas. "He was dumbfounded to see a bishop fetch wood and build a fire. . . . The church, Knoll reported, was a room, thirty feet by sixty feet, built of wood. He seemed pleasantly surprised to find that the interior at least resembled a church."[14] As Miege once told his brother: "The life of a bishop in this country is truly singular; you would without doubt laugh enough to cure any kind of illness, if I had the happiness of having you here for at least a week. I am not a merchant, and yet since I am the only one in the house who has a bit of experience, I am obliged to buy everything and to sell everything. The Americans do not take offense at this . . . ."[15]

Though Bishop Miege, man of action that he was, was not an educator he was interested in establishing Catholic schools in his vast diocese. Even before moving to Leavenworth he had begun his search for teachers. As early as 1841 the religious of the Sacred Heart, founded by the saintly Mother Philippine Duchesne, had taught school at Sugar Creek and later at Saint Mary's. There was some hope that additional help might be forthcoming. The Sisters of Loretto, who had been conducting a school for Native-American girls at the Osage Mission since 1848, also promised further help. At the time, however, Bishop Martin J. Spalding of Louisville could not spare them.[16]

While attending the provincial council of 1858 in St. Louis, Bishop Miege was blessed with a most fortunate "happening."

Opened by the Sisters of Charity in 1859 under the patronage of Our Lady of the Annunciation, this cottage at Sixth and Kickapoo streets became the first Saint Mary's Academy for Young Ladies in Leavenworth. Reprinted from McEvoy, *"Old Cathedral" Parish.*

It was there that he met Mother Xavier Ross. An agreement was soon reached whereby she and her little group of Sisters of Charity would come to Leavenworth by November 1 of that same year. These sisters, who came to be known as the Sisters of Charity of Leavenworth, were originally from Nazareth, Kentucky. In 1851 six members of the Nazareth group founded a community in the Nashville diocese. They did well until 1857, when a misunderstanding between their ecclesiastical superior, Father Ivo Schacht and Bishop Richard P. Miles, O.P., led to their departure. At the advice of some friends, Mother Ross went to St. Louis, hoping to find a bishop attending the council who might need a community of sisters in his diocese. After an interview with Archbishop Kenrick, who told her that he knew of no such bishop, she met Father De Smet, who informed her about Bishop Miège's serious need of precisely such a group.

Mother Xavier Ross paid a brief visit to Leavenworth, and in November and December the sisters moved to their new location. Mother Ross and a companion followed shortly thereafter. The sisters began teaching immediately upon arrival in Leavenworth. On March 8, 1859, they began Saint Mary's Academy for Young Ladies. Initially, classes were held in the home of Mrs. Thomas Ewing, the wife of General Ewing and sister of General William T. Sherman.[17] In the spring of 1860 a boarding school was opened in a building which the *Westport Weekly Border Star* considered to be "second only to the Planter's Hotel," the latter apparently being a top establishment. The *Border Star* also announced that the Select Boarding Academy was conducted by "ladies of the best families of the South and West, from Kentucky, Tennessee, and Maryland."[18] The brick academy building on Kickapoo Street, with its quoins, stone columns, and iron railing, was built by the bishop for six thousand dollars and rented to the sisters for fifty dollars a month. It served the academy until 1870 when the sisters built a new building where Saint Mary College now stands just outside the city.[19]

Bishop Miege realized how fortunate he was to obtain the sisters' assistance and did everything possible to accommodate them. In July 1859, he helped them establish a novitiate. Though, at first, recruits were slow to arrive, the Sisters of Charity counted twenty-seven professed religious in their group within six years. By 1858, Leavenworth had a population of ten thousand. Even so, poverty, poor living conditions, freezing winters and scorching summers, violent crime, and outbreaks of such diseases as the plague, typhus, and measles led to an increasing number of orpans. One by one these children found their way to the sisters on Kickapoo Street. When the sister's original cottage could hold no more, Bishop Miege saw to the erection of a two-story brick building across from the academy. The cost, in large part, was defrayed by the women of the city, both Catholics and Protestants, who arranged a fair that netted seven thousand dollars. The result, Saint Vincent's Orphanage, was the first of its kind in the territory. The institution was placed under the care of the Sisters of Charity of Leavenworth.[20]

During the Civil War years the Sisters of Charity also established what came to be the first civilian hospital in Kansas. Built in Leavenworth at Seventh and Kiowa streets on seven lots donated by Bishop Miege, Saint John's Hospital opened its doors on March 15, 1863. Even before the small brick building was finished, "some patients, a miserable destitute family of poor whites fleeing before Sherman's army, and without means of starting life anew, were unceremoniously and literally 'dumped' from a lumber wagon at the door." The hospital was divided into a charity ward, a public ward, and half a dozen private rooms. By summer 1863 it was already filled to capacity. Although visiting physicians were on call, patients could request the services of their family physician while in the hospital.[21]

The work done by the Sisters of Loretto at the Osage Mission and that of the Sisters of the Sacred Heart among the Potawatomi has already been mentioned. The latter group first came to Kansas in June 1841. At that time Philippine Duchesne and three younger sisters settled at Sugar Creek, where the Jesuits had founded a mission three years earlier. Their purpose was to start a school for the education of Native-American girls. The native peoples welcomed them warmly. Unfortunately, Philippine was somewhat of a failure from a practical point of view. She knew little English and had no aptitude for the Potawatomi tongue. Still, she was able to help her beloved people, especially in the areas of health care and gardening. It was not long before she became a great favorite with them. They held her in great respect not only due to her age—she was seventy-two—but also for the four hours each morning and four hours each afternoon she spent before the Blessed Sacrament. They recognized her saintly qualities, calling her Quam-kah-ka-num-ad—Woman-who-prays-always. Ill health forced Sister Philippine to leave Sugar Creek after one year to retire to St. Charles, Missouri. When the Jesuits moved the mission to Saint Mary's in 1848, the Sisters of the Sacred Heart accompanied them and continued their work. They remained at Saint Mary's until the closing of the mission.[22]

Considering the turmoil in Kansas during the Civil War years, it is amazing that the bishop made such great progress in Catholic education. In addition to the schools mentioned above, the Sisters of Charity operated another academy in Lawrence, which also had its own church and resident priest. By 1859, Saint Benedict's College had opened in Atchison. Benedictine nuns were also conducting an academy there. In May 1859, the Reverend Ivo Schacht arrived in Kansas from Tennessee, obtained some lots in Prairie City and started a church and a school. Five years after coming to Leavenworth, Bishop Miege could count fifteen priests and sixteen churches in his vicariate of Kansas. By 1864, the number of churches had risen to twenty-five.[23]

Prior to Bishop Miege's arrival in Kansas, the Jesuits from
Saint Mary's Mission frequently conducted services in and about
Fort Leavenworth in a one-story frame building that also served
as a chapel. General Michael Morgan, Chief Commissary of
Subsistence at the fort, later informed his superiors:

> This temporary chapel was also used by the regimental
> band at the post for practice. It was found that the band
> spilled their beer over the altar and that they entered the
> recess back of the altar used as a sacristy and disturbed
> what they found there. It was thought that this could eas-
> iest be mended by the Catholics putting up their own
> church edifice.[24]

In 1870, Father Ignatius Panken, S.J., suggested to Bishop
Miege that he apply to the Secretary of War for a building site
at the fort. The bishop did not delay doing so. On December
10 of the same year he addressed the Secretary of War as follows:

> Sir:
>   I beg leave to expose to your excellency that there is a
> considerable number of Roman Catholics at Fort
> Leavenworth, Kansas, to whom I consider it my duty to
> give the facilities which all Christian denominations give
> to their members.
>   Thus far it has not been possible to obtain a place or
> chapel exclusively dedicated to Catholic worship, which
> is a great inconvenience, not only to the clergyman who
> appoints days to officiate at the fort, but also to the
> members of the church. To obviate all difficulties, I take
> the liberty to ask that a piece of ground at or near the
> fort be set apart, and that the buildings erected thereon
> be for the exclusive use of Roman Catholic worship.
>   Hoping that my petition will be favorably considered,
> I remain, of your excellency, the humble obedient ser-
> vant, John B. Miege, Bishop of Kansas.[25]

General John Pope endorsed the proposition, and a board
of officers was soon given the task of selecting a site. Within a
few months, General Morgan and Ordinance Sergeant

Cornelius Kelly collected over three thousand dollars. This, together with outside help and assistance from the quarter-master's department, enabled the cornerstone to be laid in the fall of 1871. The chapel was appropriately dedicated to Saint Ignatius Loyola, the soldier-saint founder of the Society of Jesus, and served the needs of the fort until December 1889, when the present church was built.[26]

8

THE BISHOP VISITS PIKE'S PEAK

A news article headed "Gold Excitement—Pike's Peak!" in the *Leavenworth Journal* on September 11, 1858, stated that the Pike's Peak frenzy was raging fiercely in that community, threatening to carry off a number of its citizens. The *Journal* theorized that the fervor would continue to increase for a few days and then abate "like yellow fever at the approach of frost." As evidence of the "disease" the *Journal* spoke of hair being cut in "Pike's Peak style," beef served "a la mode Pike's Peak" with "Pike's Peak sauce" on one's pudding. The paper gave little encouragement, however, to those who were about to head West expecting to acquire huge piles of "Benton mint drops" taken from the ground fully coined. Rather, prospective miners tended to heed reports, published that same September 11 in the *Kansas Weekly Herald,* that eight, ten, and fifteen dollars per day had been made using the simplest tools: "those who ought to know say that with the proper tools fifty dollars can be obtained per day." By the following February, the *Chicago Press* and *Tribune* could report that: ". . . a bigger army than Napoleon conquered half of Europe with, is already equipping itself for its western march to despoil the plains of their gold. The vanguard has already passed the Rubicon, if I may so metamorphose the muddy Missouri."[1]

Bishop Miege, for his part, had to solve several problems arising out of the discovery of gold in Colorado and the ensuing

Crossing the plains, circa 1859. Source unknown.

"rush" to obtain a share of it. Eastern Colorado was part of the Kansas vicariate and, as such, was under the bishop's spiritual jurisdiction. As more and more Catholics headed for the gold fields, he felt obligated to visit the area to determine whether a resident priest was needed. Also, he wanted to become more knowledgable regarding the extent of the gold deposits, so as better to advise young Catholics whether it was worth their while to seek their fortune there.

Gold mining began in Colorado in 1858 with several small placer operations in the Denver area. Chiefly responsible for the early discoveries of gold were Green Russell and his Georgian fortune hunters. Disappointed with their findings, most of the Russell party returned home in the spring of 1859. Meanwhile, some thirty miles west of Denver, George A. Jackson came upon a valuable deposit in the mountains at Idaho Springs. Then, a few months later, in early May 1859, John H. Gregory made his famed strike on the north fork of Clear Creek, at the headwaters of the Arkansas River. With the possible exception of the Cripple Creek findings some thirty years later, the placer mines discovered in the area, called California Gulch, came to be the richest in Colorado. It is estimated that the mines at California Gulch yielded one million dollars in "dust" within two years.[2] Even before 1854, freight wagoners had been plying their trade between Missouri and the Far West. These now carried the news of the discoveries, and soon thousands of gold-hungry fortune seekers poured into Colorado from all over the United States.

Writing in February 1859, John Baptist Miege gave an interesting account of the discoveries to his brother Urban:

This past autumn gold deposits were discovered towards the western extremity of Kansas at the foot of the Rocky Mountains. According to the reports that reach us daily from these parts, those who wish to work easily pick up 25 to 50 francs a day; there are even some who speak of 1,000 francs a week. The papers have so turned peoples' heads on this topic that we expect an emigration of at least 100,000 men this spring all headed for Pike's Peak; the steamboats arrive here loaded with young folks who are going there to seek their fortune. It is not very easy to judge the outcome exactly; the general impression is that there is certainly gold there, but is there as much as they say? This is what many seem to doubt; and it is possible that there is not enough for the numbers of those who are going there. As for me, I am doing all I can to dissuade Catholics from going, quite convinced as I am that the dangers for soul and body there are just about inevitable, and that for one who succeeds there will be at least 50 who will be ruined forever.

However, so many Catholics are going to establish themselves there that I shall make a trip there next autumn to build a church and prepare a residence for a priest if his presence is necessary. It is only 200 leagues [600 miles] from Leavenworth; in two months I can fulfill the object of my mission and return home; then I shall be able to give you relatively accurate information on the gold mines of Kansas.[3]

Bishop Miege was not able to get away from Leavenworth until 1860. He began his next letter to Urban in July of that year, by telling him that his letter of May found him at the western extremity of Kansas, on the top of the Rocky Mountains, between the two glaciers that separate Kansas from Utah. He then mentioned that he left Leavenworth on the second of May with two good mules, his old carriage, a driver (Brother John Kilcullin) as well as a recently converted lawyer as a companion, and provisions for a month. The purpose of the trip was to visit any Catholics who happened to be there and to verify the reports of the recent discoveries.[4]

The route that the little party followed took them quite a bit north of Highway 70, the present direct line from Kansas City to Denver. Rather, they followed the Kaw (Kansas River) to Saint Mary's, where they made a brief stop and then continued to Fort Riley. There they veered north for three days along the Republican River. After two days they followed the Little Blue River toward Fort Kearny on the Platte River. According to the bishop, nothing much happened—except that they almost froze to death in a terrible blizzard. Still, until they left the Republican, grass, water, and wood for fire were in ample supply. Once they struck the main trail to California they found travel more difficult. For a while the water was muddy, and grass was almost nonexistent. Conditions improved once they left Fort Kearny. They had to rely on buffalo chips, which were plentiful, to start the fire and produced a flame, the bishop told his brother, "as good as the leaf mold of your mountains."[5]

The following story will give us some idea of the bishop's appearance in the course of his travels in the wild. On one occasion, when Bishop J. B. Lamy of Santa Fe was crossing the plains, his party was "surprised by the arrival in camp of a lonely stranger, with beard unshaven, wearing a summer linen coat and carrying a gun on his shoulder." He was tall and well built. While they were happy to meet an American who spoke French, they felt ill at ease at his incessant questions. He wanted to know who they were, where they were going, why they were camping during such fine weather when they should have been moving on, and so forth. At length he smiled and told them that he knew their bishop and that he himself was Bishop Miege, vicar of these parts.[6]

We need not be surprised that Bishop Miege should have looked a bit on the disreputable side at times. It was commonly known that he was always ready to do his share of camp duties, whether to gather firewood, fetch water, or care for the animals. One does not wear formal clothing on such occasions. A few years before his trip to Colorado he gave his Savoyard friend, the Abbé Marjolet, an interesting description of travel in the grasslands. The missionary who has to undertake a journey of several days, he explained, must have a sturdy horse, a good blanket, a strong line—at least three feet long—to tether the horses, and a saddle bag. On one side of the bag are the supplies that are needed to say Mass; on the other side, a bit of bread, a piece of meat, and some coffee. If he has a guide, he entrusts to him a coffee pot, two tin cups, and an axe. At sunset they will hunt for a campsite. Water and wood are needed and as soon as these are found, the horses are unsaddled, and their two feet are tied with a two- to three-foot long cord in such a way that they will not be able to wander too far off. Then one man fetches wood, the other fetches water. One of them will make a good fire and some strong coffee. There is no table to set and little to serve. Each one sits down and eats as strength or fatigue permits. After the meal comes the pipe, a bit of chatting, a review of the day, a few prayers, and bed. The latter is simple as can be. The grass serves as a mattress, the saddle a pillow, the blanket a shelter to ward off the chill of the night.

The bishop then described the rest of the evening:

No doubt you think that, after a day of rough travel in the burning heat, to cast oneself on the grass and sleep are one and the same thing. That's wrong. Never is a traveler less able to sleep than at this moment. Squadrons of mosquitos soon surround him, besiege him, torment him, hurl themselves at every unguarded post; it is a regular battle, a real massacre, where gasps and groans are as useless as the cuffs and slaps, which seem to have no more effect than to make the poor victim sweat and to multiply the number of his enemies. There is only one choice: to bury your head in the blanket, to close all openings and resign yourself to the lesser of the evils, that of sweating huge drops until dawn comes to end the torture. Then, again, as one makes the fire and coffee, the other looks for the horses and saddles them to begin again the fatigues of the previous day.[7]

What the bishop dreaded most in this type of travel was the sudden flooding of rivers. Waters could rise as much as twelve feet in one night. Only a novice would attempt to swim such a river on horseback. To make a raft would take time and would not be entirely safe either. There was nothing to do but watch the river patiently until "[He] who allows the water to rise lets it fall." Or one could travel up the torrent until reaching a ford.

Nor did the bishop have much use for rattlesnakes, which he called the "most impudent of their species." He told Marjolet that, on one occasion, he and two other horsemen gathered around a good-sized version. The creature reared up against them and shook all its rattles. For fear lest the horses be bitten, the party moved off and left "M. Rattler," as the bishop called it, the "master of the land." Miege did not sleep well that particular night—an ant bit him and other insects that landed on his head and hands seemed like so many rattlers ready to fill him with venom.[8]

Getting back to Bishop Miege's trip to Colorado, we should mention that three days out of Fort Kearny, a serious misfortune struck the bishop—he lost his best mule. Apparently the good animal became overheated and died after an attack. Fortunately, some Catholics from Leavenworth came and camped alongside the bishop's party. They had an extra horse and lent it to the bishop, who hitched it up with the remaining mule and thus was unable to reach Denver. For the most part the journey along the Platte and then down its south branch was not pleasant. At times violent sandstorms forced the party to stop for hours at a time because they could scarcely open their eyes.

The "roads" witnessed an endless stream of travelers, wrote the bishop. W. J. Howlett adds that some even "came with pushcarts, with wheelbarrows, and on foot with packs on their backs. . . ."[9] While stopping at a house, its occupants told the bishop that from May 1 to May 15 they had counted eleven thousand wagons, each with four to six men, all headed for the gold fields. He concluded: "Poor unfortunates! If they would give our Divine Master a little of the energy they show for worldly riches what a real and rich harvest they would gather." Bishop Miege arrived at Denver on May 26. On the following day, Pentecost Sunday, he delivered what he thought to be the first Mass ever said at the foot of the Rocky Mountains.[10]

Denver was a new town in May 1860. Its first settlers, John Simpson Smith and his Native-American wife, had arrived in the fall of 1857. A year later came the Russell party, the discovery of gold on Cherry Creek, and the subsequent settlements of Auraria on the West Bank and St. Charles on the East. The two settlements were united about the time of the bishop's arrival and named Denver after the territorial governor, General James W. Denver. Amazingly enough, by 1860, the tiny town already had a "store," a hotel (the Eldorado), a school of sorts, and a newspaper *(The Rocky Mountain News)*. If the famed Palace Gambling Hall and Theatre, known all over the West, were not yet in evidence we may be sure that there would have been at least one saloon to help quench the dusty throats of the miners.

On May 29, three days after arriving at Denver, the bishop set out for the mountains and, two days later, arrived at the mines. There he found, in the space of three leagues, some eight thousand men working the placer deposits of gold-bearing gravel and sand. Others were getting ready to work, but many were unable to do one or the other since they did not have a claim or could not find work. He was convinced that more than half would have traveled southward had they the means to do so. "Happily," he wrote, "I have found only a few Catholics in this place." Leaving, he returned to Denver, where the following Sunday he said Mass and preached to about one hundred people.[11] He used this occasion to meet the Catholics of Denver and devise means for building a church there.

On June 6, Bishop Miege started out on his tour of the southern part of the mines. According to Howlett, he visited California Gulch at the head of the Arkansas River. Howlett thinks that, during the course of his stay there, he would also have visited Gregory Gulch, Central City, and surrounding areas.[12] Bishop Miege described his experience to his brother as follows:

> First I went to the foot of Pike's Peak which you will find on your map. I went around this threading my way along roads frightful with rocks, with precipices, climb and descent, into the South-Park, which is a magnificent plain about 35 leagues around, entirely surrounded by mountains. There one of the wheels of my wagon broke down. Fortunately there were three other wagons in our company belonging to friends. I put the wheel in one of the wagons to have it repaired some 30 leagues further on, and put my baggage in another. I took a seat in the third, and leaving my wagon in God's care, we continued our route to the foot of the glaciers where the Arkansas takes its source.[13]

Miege explained to his brother how the Pike's Peak area contained some of the richest mines to be discovered in the

Rocky Mountains thus far. He found as many as five thousand men working a piece of land that measured six miles long and one hundred feet wide. Some of his acquaintances were taking out ore daily that was valued at five hundred to one thousand francs. At the rate of five francs to the dollar, five hundred francs would be one hundred dollars with a buying power equal to perhaps as much as two thousand dollars today. The bishop hastened to add that the number of such fortunates was limited. He stayed at the diggings for two days, heard some confessions, examined the mines, and departed for Denver. On the way, he picked up his "carriage" that, though somewhat despoiled by thieves, was still quite useable. Arriving at Denver he presented it to a friend who had shown him "much kindness."

The carriage, a gift from Father De Smet, was famous throughout the Kansas and Nebraska territories. As Miege explained, it had traveled more than fifteen hundred leagues (forty-five hundred miles), from Canada to Texas, from Leavenworth, Kansas, to the Rocky Mountains. When we consider that this wagon was once used to peddle milk in the streets of St. Louis, we can readily see why the bishop did not dare risk his return in so "venerable" a vehicle. Instead, he sold his remaining mule for 650 francs and took his place in the stagecoach that ran from Denver to Leavenworth.[14]

It is certain that the good bishop did not know what he was getting himself into or he might still have risked driving his beat-up old prairie schooner back to Leavenworth. As a young man, Mark Twain traveled west over much of the same route that Bishop Miege took back to Leavenworth. Apparently the going was not too difficult over level ground. It was the numerous brooks and creeks that caused the trouble. Usually these had high, steep banks so that the coach would "fly" down one bank and "scramble" up the other with the inevitable result that everything inside the coach became chaotic. Twain described the situation as follows:

> First we would all be down in a pile at the forward end of the stage, nearly in a sitting position, and in a second we would shoot to the other end, and stand on our heads. And we would sprawl and kick too, and ward off ends and corners of mailbags that came lumbering over

and about us; and as the dust rose from the tumult, we would all sneeze in chorus, and the majority of us would grumble, and probably say some hasty thing like: "Take your elbow out of my ribs!"[15]

The trip from Denver to Leavenworth, which took the bishop twenty-three days on the way out, was completed in six consecutive days of "trot and gallup" on the way back. Most likely the stage line that the bishop took was the one organized in the summer of 1859 by Russell and Majors. William Russell had been engaged in freighting ventures in Kansas since 1855. With the discovery of gold at the western end of the territory, there was need for a service to care for both passengers and mail. The result was the Leavenworth and Pike's Peak Express Company, which began operation on May 17, 1859. The 687-mile long route ran through the heart of Kansas, down the Smokey Hill River valley to Fort Riley and on to Leavenworth. It was the route traveled by many immigrants and later adopted by the Kansas-Pacific Railroad.[16] The fatigue resulting from a lack of sleep was so great that the bishop confessed to his brother that he could not have withstood it another twenty-four hours. He added: "After my arrival [at Leavenworth], I slept three to four days without stopping; and I took some remedies that restored my balance, and now I am just about as well as ever."

Finding it impossible to care for the western section of "Kansas"—Denver, after all, is closer to New Mexico than Leavenworth—Bishop Miege consulted with the archbishop and bishops of the St. Louis province. Accordingly, they decided to attach "the Pike's Peak country" to the Diocese of Santa Fe. The transfer was a temporary measure; confirmation would have to come from Rome to make it permanent.[17] The former vast diocese of "East of the Rockies" was thus reduced to the state of Kansas. It was with a sigh of relief that John Baptist could tell his brother that this would be his first and final trip to the mountains.[18]

9

"BLEEDING KANSAS"

In a letter of February 26, 1856, Bishop Miege informed his brother Urban that affairs were taking a turn for the worse in Leavenworth. Life was no safer than property. There had been murders without end that winter, some of them amid horrible circumstances. The bishop went on to tell his brother that, though a lover of peace, he always kept a loaded gun at the head of his bed.[1] In the midst of all this lawlessness it was almost impossible to venture forth to visit the various parishes of his diocese.

The principal cause of these disorders was the Kansas-Nebraska Act of 1854 that repealed the Missouri Compromise and made slavery illegal in the territories. Now, through popular sovereignty, the slavery question was to be determined by the residents of the Kansas and Nebraska territories, depending upon which constitution they chose. Thus, from 1854 to 1861 "bleeding Kansas" became a battleground between free-state advocates and proslavery forces.

Bishop Miege found himself in the middle. Atchison to the north came to be a rallying point for the proslavery faction, while Lawrence to the south was free-state. As early as December 1854 the bishop wrote to his brother Urban expressing the serious need for protection. "We are falling into the hands of the Philistines," he wrote. He saw little hope for religion and tranquility in the mass of newcomers arriving daily from all over the United States and Europe. There were few Catholics among the lot, and unfortunately those who were, did not practice their religion. As Bishop Miege put it they were "all covered with rust." Moreover, they were so scattered that it was difficult to visit them, let alone instruct them.[2]

Writing in Latin to the Jesuit Father General some two years later, Miege was able to say that some peace prevailed but that the future did not look promising. Fear and anxiety exceeded the hopes of the people. During the previous August—and especially the month of September—"thieves, robbers, murderers were able to do whatever they pleased with no punishment," he wrote. Because of the imminent danger from thieves and armed bands occupying most of the territory, he was unable to visit various parts of the vicariate as he had planned. Even Leavenworth itself was not safe. He mentioned how, at the insistence of friends, he had procured all kinds of weapons and used them when warranted. As an example of this he told the following story. "One night after a very agitated day because of three murders publicly committed in the city, I was indulging in a deep sleep. An unaccustomed noise outside the window awakened me. I at once went to a place from which I could perceive the cause of the noise. I saw a part of an entity which I took to belong to a thief. At once I took a gun and pointing it at the visible part I shot. But what was my amazement when I saw a pig fleeing on all feet, grunting, lacking however its tail which it left behind as a valuable trophy. Although always prepared, never after this remarkable episode have I used arms and I hope I will never be obliged to."[3]

In spite of living far from the larger cities, Bishop Miege had a solid grasp of national affairs. For example, he was able to inform his brother about the terrible drought, the ensuing scarcity, and the many bankruptcies that resulted from the depression of 1854. He was particularly outraged at the open persecution of Catholics, with churches being burned and pillaged and priests maltreated, especially in the eastern United States. He was quite likely thinking of the Know Nothing Party when he wrote: "All this is the work of that miserable secret society . . . whose members are bound under oath to oppose with all their strength strangers who have not been born in America, and especially Catholics, whether born in this country or not."[4] The Know Nothing Party became the American Party in 1854.[5]

Bishop Miege was correct in stating that the cause for nativist alarm was the influx of so many immigrants in the mid-1850s. After the famine of 1845–47 in Ireland, thousands of Irish flocked to America. Not having the means to buy farms, they gravitated toward cities like New York, Boston, and Philadelphia. The same was somewhat true of the Germans, who came here because of the political troubles in "the Germanies" about the same time. Like the Irish, many of these new settlers who came from the South German States were Catholic. It is surprising how soon some of these "foreigners" were able to assume rather prominent positions in politics, business, and the professions in their adopted land. As Miege further notes, by 1855 the American Party had gained a degree of political success, carrying "almost all the elections in each state." Actually, they won the governorship, or legislature, or both in four New England states as well as in Maryland, Kentucky, and California. They were almost as successful in the South. The bishop turned out to be somewhat of a prophet when he concluded, "We do not fear their threats; a bit of persecution will do us no harm; and after two or three years we will be more at ease and stronger than ever."

By 1856 the American Party had given way to the new Republican Party. It is not surprising that the German Catholics in Kansas, by then quite numerous, should have shunned the new party. The Democrats, they felt, were more sympathetic toward Catholic rights. Father Heimann, the onetime missionary at Saint Mary's, noted that the Republicans were Northerners and in many ways resembled the rabble-rousing Red Republicans and Forty-eighters of Europe. In the North, ministers preached violence against slaveholders while advocating "extirpation of the pope and papists." Heimann refers to some members of the party as being "the bitterest enemies of our Holy Faith." Little wonder, then, that the Catholic settlers in Kansas, many of whom were immigrants, should have considered nativism and similar anti-Catholic movements more pressing than that of slavery.[6] Finally, public opinion in the United States never did accept the Know

Nothing Party's estimate of immigrants nor of Catholic citizens. About the only bit of its political philosophy that has endured is opposition by some to denominational schools.

Kansas was granted statehood on January 29, 1861. The *Leavenworth Times* greeted the occasion with an editorial that was brief, dignified, and somewhat poetic:

> The long agony is over. The dream of years is realized. Justice, tardy but ever certain, has been meted out to the people, and this soil which they have chosen as their heritage is embraced within the charmed circle of a state sovereignty, distinct and yet reciprocal. The field of blue upon our national flag is to be embellished with another star, the luster of whose orb we predict will vie with the fairest of the constellation. The last act of the drama which opened in blood and was continued in violence has been enacted and the curtain has fallen upon a happy consummation long desired and long postponed. We trust our history as a state may be as brilliant as the struggle and trials of our territorial condition has been severe and aggravated. If such shall be the case, Kansas will stand in the records of the future without a peer.[7]

Unfortunately, statehood did not bring an end to the drama of blood and violence. For Kansas the outbreak of the Civil War in 1861 was to mean almost four years of harassment by bandits and by freebooters espousing the cause of the South. From the beginning, Lawrence had been a center of free-state activities, which resulted in the town being sacked, on May 21, 1856, five years before the war began. The fortified Free State Hotel and the two antislavery newspapers, *Herald of Freedom* and *Kansas Free State* were destroyed on that day.[8] The violence continued during the Civil War. Some three hundred guerrillas under the leadership of William Quantrill reached Lawrence at 5:00 A.M. on the morning of August 21, 1863. The town was put to the torch. Two hundred buildings were destroyed and about 150 lives lost. It has been called "the blackest crime recorded in American history."

We are told by author Watler E. Connelly that

> A cordon had been thrown about the city and every avenue of escape closed. The survivors of that awful day

said that guerilla guards seemed to rise out of the ground, so quickly and thoroughly were they stationed . . . . Fiery liquors from plundered shops were poured down thirsty throats, and the band became a drunken mob. Demoniac yells rose above the crackling of pistol-shots . . . drunken guerillas rode recklessly through the principal streets firing wildly and shouting in exultation for Quantrill, Jeff Davis, and the Southern Confederacy. Other bands bent on murder went about their business with method and dispatch.[9]

Why all this hatred? Some of the raiders were likely retaliating. Some may have been wronged and were seeking revenge. But deeper still ran the roots of hatred sprung from the slavery struggles of the preceding years. "And it remained for Quantrill," writes Connelly, "a man who cared nothing for slavery as an institution, nothing for the abolition of slavery, nothing for the North, nothing for the South, to seize upon this feeling and make it a means to gratify his thirst for blood and greed for spoil and plunder."[10]

Bishop Miege had come to Lawrence the day before the massacre with two of his priests in order to administer the sacrament of confirmation. On August 21 he was staying with Father Sebastian Favre, the local pastor at the time. Quantrill entered the house and asked the Fathers if they had anything to eat. They said they had some cheese, some bread and butter, and that he was welcome to them. We are told that Quantrill "was pleased with their kind simplicity and sat down to eat." Just then some of his men shot a citizen out in front of the priest's house. The bishop saw him fall and asked Quantrill if it was safe to offer assistance. Quantrill replied that he doubted it, but Bishop Miege was already on his way. He leaned close to the poor fellow, spoke a few words, and anointed him. The dying man was conscious and, grasping the bishop's hand to his bosom, breathed his last.[11] After the raid Bishop Miege gave the last rites to a dozen or more of Quantrill's victims.[12] Fortunately, the Fathers escaped injury, and the church escaped the flames. Bishop Miege returned to Leavenworth soon after the raid.

While the war brought some annoyance to the citizens of Leavenworth, according to Father Francis X. De Coen, S.J., assistant to Bishop Miege during the war, conditions

Sketch of the ruins of Lawrence, Kansas. Courtesy
Kansas State Historical Society, Topeka, Kansas.

remained comparatively quiet in the city itself, perhaps due
to the large number of Union soldiers present. There were
about three thousand troops in the city in addition to those at
the fort. Still, their very presence precipitated the only incident of any importance that affected the church in
Leavenworth during the war. When the Ninth Wisconsin
Regiment, entirely made up of German refugees from the
troubles of 1848, arrived in Leavenworth they were quartered
in Saint Joseph's Church on the sole authority of one of the
officers. The pastor was ill at the time, and the bishop was
making his annual retreat. Father De Coen did what he could
to have the soldiers ousted, but apparently with little success.
As soon as he heard of the affair, Bishop Miege went to the
fort to complain to the general, who then ordered the immediate arrest of the officers, evacuation of the church, and payment for all damages sustained.[13]

Bishop Miege strongly recommended his priests to have
nothing to do in word or deed with the politics of the different parties. For the most part, they obeyed. Father Ponziglione
relates that the bishop's house was "a real neutral ground and
safe harbor where friend and foe could meet without any
danger." Army officers as well as private citizens could see
him at will and seemed to rely on his counsel and advice.
About a year after Quantrill's raid on Lawrence, when General
Sterling Price's Missouri expedition threatened to attack
Leavenworth, all able-bodied men were called on to defend
the city.[14] Father Ponziglione and another priest volunteered
their services, but they were told to remain with the bishop
and go wherever need would call them.[15]

Kansas was far removed from the center of the war. What danger existed came chiefly from roaming bands of border ruffians. While things remained relatively quiet in Leavenworth, this was not true elsewhere. As Father De Coen wrote: "In our goodly state of Kansas, moveable property, such as money, horses, mules, and the like, is changing hands very briskly." Confederate sympathizers raided Union men, and the latter returned the compliment. Some fought "under both flags, as occasion may be;" they plundered Union men one day and "seceshers" the next. De Coen referred to this situation as an old Kansas institution.[16] Apparently it was not enough to be a loyal Union man in Kansas since abolitionists persecuted all Democrats, especially if they were Irish—the Irish were known to be staunchly Democratic and thus especially subject to suspicion.[17] Nor were the Jesuit missionaries free from harm. When Father Schoenmakers attempted to secure the loyalty of the Quapaw Indians to the Union, Confederate sympathizers threatened his life, and the father had to take refuge at Saint Mary's. Fathers Ponziglione and James Van Goch also had encounters with soldiers, who would not have hesitated to shoot them had not several half-breeds and a saber captain interceded.[18] Presumably, Kansas *jayhawkers*—antislavery guerrillas—and Missouri *bushwhackers*—proslavery guerrillas—robbed and killed each other "to their heart's content." If average citizens kept their mouths shut, they would not be molested. Still, in one settlement north of Parkville, Missouri, "standing chimneys, weeping women and children, were seen in every direction," with almost every second house burned down.[19]

War was not the only problem. When the Reverend Anton Kuhls, for many years pastor of Saint Mary's Church in Wyandotte, first arrived in that city in October 1864, he found "liquor to be the principal stock in trade." Natives and whites vied with each other to see who "could destroy most of [the] commodity." He tells us that during his first year, six of his parishioners "died a violent death in liquor, and many of the old settlers went to their graves with broken bones caused by liquor escapades." Apparently, the saloons were doing a thriving business but, according to the good father, not one of the owners had "prospered or transmitted his wealth to his descendants or the second generation. Some seven or eight died in the poor house, and some died by their own hands."[20]

Kuhls referred to the character of the people as "real western"—open, lighthearted, and generous. He added: "A religious bigot in those early years was a *curiosum.* Weeds—such as 'know-nothings' and A.P.As [American Protective Associations]—did not grow in our soil."[21] There were few lawyers in Wyandotte County and seemingly little need for them. One of the father's parishioners, John Link, was marshal of a public committee that administered "justice," which was meted out in summary fashion. Criminals and vagabonds were horsewhipped and given twenty-five minutes to leave town. Under such circumstances, a jail was hardly necessary.

One would like to think that Kansas settled down to law and order after the war. This was not always the case. Writing as late as 1872 Father Ponziglione bewailed conditions. "Unfortunately," he wrote, "morality is frequently a *desideratum* in many of our new towns, and no wonder for the full measure of iniquity seems to pour in upon us from the oldest and most substantial cities of this great continent. To give you an idea of this, I shall simply state what I was told while in Newton [Kansas] last summer, that of the thirty-six persons buried in that place, only one had died a natural death. Such is the field which we are working."[22]

Up to 1869 the vicariate had no residence west of Junction City, about sixty miles west of Topeka. Shortly thereafter residences were established at Salina, Hayes City, and elsewhere, but, with the exception of Abilene, these extended a hundred miles and more westward. Not at all surprising was the statement common in Kansas: "There is no Sunday west of Junction City and no God west of Salina."[23]

If turmoil during the war caused settlers to avoid Kansas, the comparative tranquility of the postwar years changed all that. Kansas was to be deluged with immigrants. Bishop Miege ascribed this influx to the benefits of the Homestead Act of 1862. He wrote:

We have millions of acres of good unoccupied land, and the immigrants can take possession of it without paying anything to the government. They are rushing out here in great numbers and there are many Catholics among them. Those who are good and willing to work are wealthy in a few years.[24]

Under the Homestead Act, which granted 160 acres of land to each settler, 100 million acres were ultimately brought into cultivation. It is estimated that in Kansas, Nebraska, Minnesota, and the Dakotas, more than half of the 240,000 new farms settled between 1863 to 1880 were on Homestead Act lands. By 1870 the population of Kansas had surged to 364,399.[25]

A further reason for the influx into Kansas was railroad construction, which boomed after the war ended. Important lines at the time were the Kansas Pacific (Union Pacific), Kansas City, Lawrence, and Southern (Santa Fe), and the Missouri Pacific. By 1874 Kansas alone had 2,215 miles of track crossing and crisscrossing the state. Peter Beckman points out that this development influenced the Catholic Church in Kansas in several important ways. A large number of men in the construction gangs that built the railroads were Catholic. Missionary Father Phillip Colleton claimed to have visited fifteen to twenty such construction camps in a single month, hearing confessions well into the night.[26]

The railroads helped the missionaries considerably since they enabled them to get from one place to another much more readily. As Father Ponziglione noted in his journal, though the horse still had its use, the Fathers now rode "as gentlemen in palatial cars."[27] This was a great advantage to a missionary who served several stations along a railroad right-of-way. Many of the construction workers later settled at points along the railroad, which they served in various positions. Others simply settled down and farmed the land.

By 1873, shortly before Bishop Miege retired from his office, there were fifty-five churches scattered throughout Kansas with an additional seven under construction. Further, there were some eighty-two stations without churches.[28] In these latter places, the missionary, making his rounds, would generally spend the night in the home of one of his flock, frequently a one-room shanty or dugout that housed the settler and his family. Hotels of a sort did exist at the time, but as Father Ponziglione explained, they were "places where one must not try to stop, if he can help it, for the most wicked set of people are frequently there to be found." The food of these pioneer families consisted mainly of cornbread and homemade sorghum. According to Ponziglione, the people had no trouble keeping "Fridays, or Lent, or Ember days," since meat on their tables was "a matter of rare occurrence." The missionary was generally so hungry that he gratefully accepted whatever his host could offer.[29]

The three letters written by Father Ponziglione to Missouri Provincial Father Thomas O'Neil present an excellent example of the territory covered by a Kansas missionary at the time. Some of the towns mentioned as he moved westward on his rounds were Independence, Eureka, Arkansas City, Winfield, Augusta, El Dorado, Newton, and Hutchinson. From his starting point in southwestern Kansas this would have given him a parish about 150 miles east to west and 70 miles north to south.[30] Mostly he traveled alone and by horse; at times Father Ponziglione was able to use the Atchison, Topeka, and Santa Fe Railroad. Once arriving at a station, the usual procedure was to send word out that Mass would be said. In addition, confessions were heard, baptisms administered, and marriages performed. Frequently, the little settlements were composed primarily of a particular ethnic group, such as folks of Irish, German, or French descent.[31]

10

BUILDING A CATHEDRAL

Once the turmoil in the Territory began to settle a bit, Bishop Miege was able to resume the routine visitations of his diocese. Travel remained difficult, and parish rectories were not as comfortable then as they are today. As an example of this, the Reverend Anton Kuhls, one-time pastor of Saint Mary's Church in Kansas City, Kansas, tells the following delightful story:

> The first year of my career in this place |1864| I had only one room and one small lounge. Two distinguished visitors came one afternoon, no one less than Bishop Miege and his old friend, Bishop Lamy, of Santa Fe, N. M. For supper we had a cup of coffee, some cold ham and bread. I sent to the Garno House, our only hotel, for a night's lodging for my guests. They talked over their western experiences and smoked a cigar but made no move to start for the hotel. I remonstrated with them as best I could, pointing to my scanty lounge two feet wide, as inadequate for a man of 280 pounds—the weight of Bishop Miege. All to no purpose. They declared they were provided for. At 10 o'clock P.M. they went to the chapel to say their night prayers. When through they came back, turned two chairs on the floor for pillows or

head rests and both stretched their tired limbs on the
hard wooden floor. Bishop Lamy turned a good many
times, but the Bishop east of the Rocky mountains stood
it like a brave soldier, occasionally giving his partner a
gentle digging with his elbow, telling him to be quiet for
fear of waking the sick father—meaning your humble servant who was suffering with bilious fever. I heard it just
the same, for such an heroic act of mortification kept me
from sleeping and was the best and most impressive sermon ever preached to me on practical mortification. May
God bless them both! Noble souls![1]

Father Kuhls, who knew Bishop Miege well, tells another
story that gives additional insight into the bishop's personality.
It seems that, shortly after the incident mentioned above,
Bishop Miege visited Saint Mary's on his way to Shawneetown
to administer the sacrament of confirmation. Father Kuhls proposed sending to Kansas City, Missouri, for a carriage since
there was none to be had in town at that time. "Oh no," said
the bishop, "Mr. John Waller has two mules and a lumber
wagon. Put a rocking chair in it, and the carriage is ready for
the bishop." And so it was. Meanwhile, the folks at
Shawneetown had arranged a royal welcome for his arrival.
The story continues:

Some thirty farmers came on horseback to meet the
Bishop. They passed the lumber wagon and the old gentleman with the white duster, not suspecting this to be
the Bishop. On they galloped and went as far as the Kaw
river without finding the Bishop. When they returned to
Shawnee they saw the man in the white duster sitting out
doors smoking a cigar. He was so well pleased with this
little adventure that he treated all the riders with a cigar.
It was a great treat and all enjoyed it, except the man at
the cannon, who was to fire the cannon as soon as the
Bishop came in sight. He made up for it the next day, firing the cannon to his heart's content.[2]

We may well appreciate Bishop Miege's willingness to sit in
a rocking chair on a lumber wagon when we consider his
"large frame" and his 280 pounds. Still, in spite of his size we
are told that he remained "an exceptionally handsome man."[3]

Bishop Miege was respected and loved by all who knew him in Leavenworth. He liked people, and they apparently realized this. It was only natural that, as he sat on his porch in the cool of a summer evening, folks would stop for a moment to chat with him. His "palace" as it stands today would seem to have been very large for his time. But the bishop wanted it spacious enough to accommodate his priests when they came to visit him or when they came to recover from the fatigue of their missionary work. As he told his brother, "I am happy to be able henceforth to offer them suitable hospitality, and I have them visit me once a month. This gives me the occasion to encourage them, to look into their way of acting, and their fidelity to their spiritual exercises; it is their one support in the midst of trials. When they are ill and until they are well again, I keep them with me to take care of them."[4] He took to heart the advice that Father General Roothaan gave him on his appointment as bishop. "I am sure," Roothaan wrote, "that you will avoid the *dominans in cleris* [lording it over the clergy], that you will rather be *forma factus gregis ex animo* [making a pattern of the flock from the heart]. You will think not only of the mission, but also and above everything else, of the missionaries, so as to preserve them *in utroque homine* [spiritually and materially]. You will be also their religious Superior. See to it that your government be spiritual, mild, exact, *suaviter et fortiter* [gentle and firm]."[5]

In spite of all the turmoil, the decade from 1857 to 1867 found Leavenworth in the heyday of its prosperity. With a population of twenty-five thousand, it was the largest town in Kansas, and it seemed that it might well remain so. James Meline, traveler of note, visited Leavenworth in 1866 and found no lack of hotels there, among them the Tremont, Everett, Planters, and Astor. He wrote: "Immense numbers of teams and wagons for transportation of merchandise from government stores in Utah, New Mexico, Nebraska and Montana are fitted out here, giving employment to a small army of drivers, merchants and contractors."[6] Writing in January 1867, Bishop Miege told his brother that the Catholic population of the town had increased considerably.[7] It appeared to be an opportune time to begin building the cathedral the bishop had long been planning.

As early as 1859, the Abbé Pillon, editor of the French publication *Rosier de Maria,* volunteered to canvas his subscribers for funds to build an edifice for Bishop Miege in honor of the Immaculate Conception. He suggested that the bishop visit France where he might obtain "considerable alms." Miege wrote to Cardinal Barnabo, Prefect of the Propaganda, telling him about the proposition, but the cardinal, after consulting with Jesuit Father General Beckx, refused the necessary permission. The Abbé Pillon apparently began a drive for funds on his own, since Bishop Miege was able to tell his brother in November 1860, that the good M. Pillon had already sent him forty-two thousand francs. He added that he would not begin building until he had saved 150,000 francs in order to avoid a sudden work stoppage due to trouble in Europe or revolution in the United States.[8] Since coming to Kansas, Bishop Miege had been relying on the annual grants sent to him by the Propaganda of the Faith. During the years 1861 to 1865 alone these grants totaled 119,000 francs. Since this amount was in gold, it was all the more valuable. During the war the Union issued four hundred million in "greenbacks." By August 31, 1865, $100 in gold could buy $144.25 in greenbacks. Since a cheap dollar meant higher prices, we need not wonder why the bishop should have complained at the cost of labor and building materials.[9]

In July 1862, Bishop Miege told his brother he would begin the foundations of his church the following year, but, for various reasons, excavations were delayed until the spring of 1864. Earlier, the bishop suffered a severe loss when his Jesuit companion Father De Coen died. He had sent the father to Saint Mary's to recover from an attack of asthma, which had been wearing him down. There, one day, he was found dead in his room. The bishop wrote to his brother: "Since he was a good architect and a good financier, I had given him the superintendence of my new church; and now look at me all of a sudden plunged more deeply than ever in temporal matters, without hope of being delivered. This good Father was like a brother to me; he had my trust and he really merited it."[10] In this same letter the bishop complained about the huge costs involved. The salary of a mason and a stonecutter was twenty francs a day. He had already paid forty thousand francs for the foundation of the church, and hardly half of it was completed. At the same time drought was being felt in many of the states, and there was fear of famine not because of poor harvests but due to inflationary prices.[11]

The cornerstone of the new cathedral was solemnly laid on September 18, 1864. Two days later the *Leavenworth Daily Times* stated that two or three thousand people assembled that Sunday afternoon at the corner of Fifth and Miami streets to watch the impressive ceremonies. After services at the church, the people proceeded to the stands where the ceremonies were to take place. The Reverend Father John Hennessey, future bishop of Dubuque, Iowa, delivered the sermon. The crowd then gathered around to watch the cornerstone as it was set in place and adjusted, while a band played "several lively tunes." The bishop blessed the stone with holy water and recited several prayers. The *Times* continued: "On the stone is a finely cut representation of a cross, surmounted with the date. . . . The ceremonies ended by the choir singing a beautiful hymn, the band playing the accompaniment."[12]

The design for the building was made by L. L. Long, a prominent Baltimore architect, known for his many fine churches and buildings. Unfortunately, Mr. Long did not live to see the cathedral completed.[13] The contractor of the cathedral and the rectory was James Andrew McGonigle, a member of the Cathedral parish who had come to Leavenworth from the north of Ireland in May 1857. McGonigle was recognized as one of the outstanding contractors in the Midwest. Among other buildings he constructed were a courthouse at Platte City, Missouri, part of the statehouse in Topeka, Kansas, and post offices in St. Joseph, Missouri. On first arriving in Kansas, McGonigle made the acquaintance of Bishop Miege, who entrusted the construction of the cathedral to him from foundation to completion.[14] McGonigle was later to write:

> The Bishop possessed an artistic and architectural mind, which the great work he accomplished shows. The architectural proportions of the cathedral are perfect. The sanctuary is the largest of any cathedral in this country. He often remarked that he wanted a large one so that the largest ceremonies of the church could be held with comfort. Bishop Miege secured the best fresco artist in the United States, Leon Pomarède. The figures in fresco

are perfect and even today the expressions and colors
are good. The stained glass figures show that they were
made by a first-class artist, as the colors are as fresh and
clear today as when executed thirty-seven years ago. The
cathedral is of the Romanesque style of architecture and
has no superior of that style in this country. The size of
the cathedral is 94 feet front, and 200 feet long and
about 65 feet high to square of building. The towers
when completed will be about l90 feet high.[15]

In 1865, finding himself short of funds, Bishop Miege sent
Father James Defouri to Europe on a fund-raising tour. The
commission was a success, and at the end of the year Defouri
returned with sufficient funds to allow the bishop to continue
his building program. Better still, in the course of his travels in
Savoy and Italy, Defouri was able to enlist the services of several clerics, whom he brought back with him to Kansas.[16]

While Bishop Miege was thus occupied, he received a sum-
mons to attend the Second National Council of Baltimore. He
wrote to the apostolic delegate, Martin J. Spalding, explaining
that he could not attend, since the good Lord had sent him a
"very troublesome swelling of his feet, called dropsy, which
required regular treatment." He added that he had an infirmity
that would not permit him to go as far as Baltimore. Then,
too, there was the matter of the cathedral currently under construction. He concluded by asking His Grace for a favor,
namely, to present through the national council his resignation to Rome so that he might spend "the very few remaining
years" of his life in the Society of Jesus and "do penance for
the many blunders and imperfections" of his last fifteen years.
The letter of resignation addressed to the Fathers of the
General Council reads as follows:

The undersigned, after mature deliberation, considers it
his duty to present to the Most and Right Reverend
Fathers of the Second National Council of Baltimore his
resignation of the office and dignity of Vicar Apostolic of
Kansas. His reasons are 1. Ill health caused by rhumatism
[sic], dropsy and ashma [sic], which do not permit him to
fulfill the duties of his office. 2. The increasing responsi-
bilities of the Vicariate are a burden to which his capabil-

ity and strength are unequal. 3. His failing health admon-
ishes him to prepare to meet his God, and he firmly
hopes that it will be granted him to do so by resuming
his former manner of life in the Society of Jesus.[17]

Meanwhile, in January 1867, Bishop Miege was able to
inform his brother that the church was soon to receive a protective covering. He had to obtain slates as well as slaters
from St. Louis, since up to that date the cathedral was the
only slate-roofed building in town. He also reported that he
had made a deal with his faithful in Leavenworth, whereby
he would pay for the brick work—that is, the walls and
arches of the church—and they would pay for the roof and
the outside cornices. His cost would be 225,000 francs; their
portion 100,000.[18] The bishop apparently sent his brother a
picture of the church since he wrote in August 1868: "I am
glad that the view of my church pleases you." He indicated
that the frescos, the windows, and the main altar were completed but that he still had to obtain benches, confessionals,
an organ, and two side altars. He hoped to have the solemn
dedication take place on December 8 of that year, the feast of
the Immaculate Conception.[19]

Bishop Miege had his wish fulfilled. The solemn dedication of the cathedral took place as planned. Despite an early
winter freeze, with roads blocked by drifting snow, thousands of people came to Leavenworth. Archbishop Peter
Kenrick of St. Louis dedicated the cathedral; Bishop Miege
was celebrant at the Mass. In attendance were Bishop John
Hennessey of Dubuque, who delivered an address at the
evening services, Bishop Hogan of St. Joseph, who drove
across the Missouri River on ice-slicked roads, and Bishop
James O'Gorman, Miege's successor in the vicariate of
Nebraska.[20] The address was delivered by the Reverend P. J.
Ryan of St. Louis, later Archbishop of Philadelphia, who was
noted for his oratorical prowess. The sermon, which was
delivered "in an eloquent manner," according to the
Leavenworth Daily Times, lasted over an hour. The *Times*
also went on to say that the Pontifical High Mass and sermon together was held from eleven A.M. to two P.M.—
"a very unpleasant three hours on account of the cathedral
being so cold." It is not surprising to learn that while the

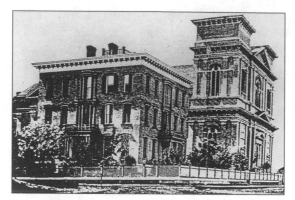

Early photo of the Cathedral of the Immaculate
Conception and *(foreground)* bishop's residence,
circa 1875. The church served as the cathedral for
the diocese until 1947, when the See city was
moved from Leavenworth to Kansas City, Kansas.
Photograph by E. E. Henry.

church was initially crowded "to its utmost capacity, the
number decreased before the service was over."[21]

What was surprising was that the vespers ceremony that
evening should have witnessed a well-filled edifice at all.
Archbishop Kenrick officiated at the ceremony, and Bishop
Hennessey delivered "a forcible sermon on the 'Head of the
Church' which was well received, though the severe cold rendered the audience restless and noisy." The *Times* was high in
its praise of the music presented during the ceremonies,
which featured the Fort Band and Choir, a choir "of adults,"
and a forty-voice children's choir. The *Times* stated: "Taken
altogether we have never had in Leavenworth a more successful combination of vocal and instrumental music; and we
hope to see the same performers on some future occasion."[22]
The *Times* concluded its description of the consecration ceremonies as follows: "Thus ended the consecration of the finest
Cathedral west of St. Louis. It will stand for ages a monument
of the business ability of Bishop Miege, and a testimony of
the energy of the Catholic Church. . . . It is an ornament to
the city and the pride of the Catholics who have contributed
to its erection."

Bishop Miege could be proud of his new cathedral and all
Leavenworth with him. Despite its rounded arches and

Interior of the Cathedral of the Immaculate
Conception, Leavenworth, Kansas, 1939. Source
unknown.

vaults and generally Romanesque style, the cathedral, in true
Jesuit manner, made profuse use of ornamentation so that it
had a distinct Baroque spirit. The high altar, for example,
was definitely Baroque. Years later, the Swedish-born mural
artist Oscar Ericson, seeing the cathedral murals for the first
time, remarked:

> It was certainly a pleasure to me, and a rare find, indeed,
> to discover, here in the Cathedral of Leavenworth, paint-
> ings by the artist Leon Pomrade [Pomaréde]. Some sixty
> years or so ago, when the Cathedral was painted, Artist
> Pomrade [Pomaréde] was one of the outstanding artists,
> if not the outstanding artist of this country. His murals
> are of the highest standard of quality and a rare exhibi-
> tion of a true artist's skill. . . . It is rather a shame to think
> that our American public often goes to the farthest points
> of Europe to find works of art that are to be found in the
> Cathedrals and churches there, and pass by, here in this
> country, works such as this which, literally speaking, is

right at their own front door, and that represent the finest
that is to be found in any Cathedral or Church anywhere.[23]

Almost a century later in the early morning of December 30,
1961, fire broke out in the cathedral. When the Leavenworth
firefighters arrived in subzero weather shortly after 1 A.M., the
edifice was already engulfed in smoke. By late morning only
the shell of the former cathedral remained standing. Rebuilding
would have been unrealistic. The remnants were razed to make
way for the modern building that now stands on its site.[24]

—— 11 ——
BISHOP MIEGE AND VATICAN COUNCIL I

Shortly before the dedication of the cathedral, Bishop Miege wrote to Urban to tell him that, when all was done, he would "give a mission" for a month, and then would take a much needed rest. He hoped to be able to visit his brother and forget the troubles of Kansas along the charming promenades of La Forêt. The bishop then added: "These are my plans; but man proposes and God disposes; it goes without saying that we completely carry out his holy will."[1]

Meanwhile a document arrived in Leavenworth that summoned all the bishops of the Catholic world to the Vatican Council, whose opening date was set for December 8, 1869. There was felt to be a real need for such a meeting. No general council had been held since the Fathers met at Trent in the sixteenth century. In the interim, such secular movements as liberalism, naturalism, socialism, atheistic evolution, and materialism had caused the Catholic Church no end of trouble. While the papacy had condemned many of these teachings in letters to the faithful as well as in a *Syllabus of Errors,* there was a general feeling that clarification was needed of certain disputed points. Hence, when the announcement of the forthcoming Council was made on June 29, 1867, there was, for the most part, considerable rejoicing among Catholics, lay as well as clergy.

Bishop Miege informed his brother that he would leave America in September 1869 and then take a few days rest with his family at Chevron. He then added: "If I go to Rome, I shall make a terrible attempt that they give me time to prepare for death. . . . "[2]

Possibly about the time of the Council, a letter without address or date, and thought to have been written by Miege to Propaganda citing the bishop's reasons for resignation, was written. The letter begins by pointing out that Miege had not wanted the episcopal office in the first place but that he accepted it out of obedience since it dealt with the conversion of an indigenous population to Christianity. Such conditions, mused Miege, were no longer valid. With the opening of the Indian Territory to white settlers in 1854, some 500,000 newcomers established towns throughout the Territory, slowly driving out the natives. Consequently, Miege felt that the vicariate should be replaced by an episcopal see in the ordinary sense of the term. Whether or not that ever came to pass, the point remained that the burden of catering to the spiritual health of thousands had been too great for Miege to bear. As a result of almost twenty years of labor, the bishop's health had broken down. Enfeebled as he was, he found it difficult to cover an area six hundred miles long and three hundred miles wide. Moreover, he maintained, the youthful diocesan priests of his vicarage needed a younger bishop to set an example. Finally, Miege concluded, there was no longer any reason for a Jesuit to be vicar since the two missions of the Society among the Potawatomi and the Osages "will soon be reduced to the level of the normal civil life" of the country.[3]

From the *Leavenworth Commercial* we learn of a "most interesting and impressive scene" that took place at the bishop's residence on Wednesday, September 15, 1869. A large number of priests laboring in the diocese arrived there, anxious that "some mark of their love and veneration for their bishop should be shown before he proceded to Rome to attend the Ecumenical Council." The group was introduced by Father Himos, who presented to the bishop on their behalf a beautiful gold cross and chain, made in St. Louis specially for the occasion. He then addressed the bishop as follows:

Beloved Bishop:

Knowing that the day of your departure for the Eternal City is drawing nigh, and anticipating already the feeling of loneliness that will dwell in our hearts during your absence from amongst us, we the clergy of your Vicariate have hastened hither . . . to present a small token of love and veneration, and to cheer and comfort you on the eve of a long and arduous journey, by reminding you of the golden links of strong affection existing between you and your priests.

We call to mind kind words of encouragement which have often gladdened us amidst the laborious duties of the mission.

We have learned to feel that a paternal heart yearned for our success, and we have often thanked God for having placed in this distant portion of his vinyard [sic] a spiritual ruler who possesses the noblest, the most exalted virtues.[4]

The address further reminded the bishop of the many good works he had done in his vicariate and concluded with a promise of fervent prayers for him during his absence. We are told that the bishop "had great difficulty in overcoming his emotion, and was evidently much affected, even to tears, at this mark of love shown to him by the priests of his Vicariate." It took him several minutes to compose himself in order to thank them for this proof of their affection. We might add here that, during the night, the old leaden cross he was in the habit of wearing was removed from his room, so that he was obliged to wear the one presented to him.

The last twenty years of labor in his vicariate, his difficult travels, his concern for his flock, his ocean voyages, and his financial problems had done much to lessen his former robust constitution. His relatives and friends back home noted the change. As Garin was to point out, he suffered greatly from severe asthma, and a sore throat prevented any lengthy discourse. He was also plagued with frequent fits of gout in his feet, no doubt the result of an unbalanced diet, especially while traveling in the wilderness of the Indian Territory. Little wonder then that his friends found their venerable compatriot quite elderly looking. After a lengthy summary of Miege's work, Garin concludes: "His stature always remained impressive, but his legs had trouble supporting his body, which was weighed down by ill health; his voice was quite weak and his one-time cheerfulness singularly diminished; this was no longer the amiable storyteller of 1853."[5]

After a few days rest with his family and friends, Bishop Miege took the road to Rome the first week in November. He arrived there considerably before the opening of the Council, since he wanted to discuss with Pius IX the state of his vicariate and his own personal position. The pope received with kindness his beloved vicar apostolic, whom he had known personally for such a long time. Although the bishop earnestly begged to be relieved—at least in part—from his pastoral duties, the pope felt compelled to postpone his decision. The bishop, ever resigned to God's will, submitted humbly to this new delay and went about preparing for the forthcoming Vatican Council.[6] While in Rome he stayed at the Gesù, mother church of the Jesuits.

Fortunately, we have a few of the letters that Bishop Miege wrote from Rome at the time of the Council. They are valuable since they give his views on some of the happenings and, thus, add to the history of the gathering. But they also serve to show that he was fully aware of the political motivation that prompted some of its members to act as they did; that is, the letters give us some idea of the attitude of the prelate during the Council, particularly regarding faith, morals, the discipline of the Church, and the question of papal infallibility.

In preparing for the Council, a committee of five cardinals was appointed to draw up an agenda. Aided by theologians, canon lawyers, and other specialists, the cardinals, following the proceedings of Trent, assigned two series of topics to be addressed. The first concerned the Catholic faith and the second the organization of the Church. Each contained several chapters to be discussed and voted on by the Fathers.[7]

The first series, or *schemata,* as they were called, involved church doctrine and made for almost endless debates, often quite heated. Some five hundred amendments resulted. Bishop Miege called these sessions, which were quite repetitious, "very fatiguing." "But," in typically obedient fashion, he added, "it is always a pleasure to attend them."[8] Actually, the differences did not center on the doctrines as such but rather on the wording of the document as a whole. For example, one question raised was whether materialistic doctrines should be attacked "directly and by name" or whether a more prudent method should be used.[9] When put to a final vote on April 24, 1870, the first schemata on matters of faith were unanimously adopted by the Fathers of the Council. This redefining of Catholic doctrine in the light of the philosophies of the day—rationalism, naturalism, indifferentism, pantheism—was a valuable contribution of Vatican Council I.[10]

In a letter to his friend Canon Alliaudi, Bishop Miege referred to the Council as a "world of men 55 to 80 years old, almost all of them old laborers in the vineyard of the Lord, who love the Church and venerate the Pontiff who governs it." He added: "You have there all the appearances, all the costumes, all colors of beards, all the differences of language." He noted that the Latin language used throughout the Council was understood by all, except for a few Asians, who used interpreters. He then offered an interesting observation. "You have there all the Oriental majesty, the French and Italian elegance and gravity, the American lack of ceremony, the German ponderousness, the Spanish vivacity. In a word, it is beautiful . . . but one should be able to describe it and have the time to do so; both of these are lacking for me."[11]

The real trouble for the Council began on January 21, 1870, when the schemata on the nature of the Church were submitted for discussion. Among the topics were some highly controversial matters, such as the rights and duties of the civil powers and church-state relations. For some time, in and out of the Council, the bishops had been arguing over the proposition defining the infallibility of the papacy. Two parties soon formed. Those who favored the definition of papal infallibility were led by such stalwarts as Victor Auguste Dechamps of Belgium and Henry Edward Manning of England and were backed by a majority of the Fathers. For the most part those who opposed the definition were led by Félix Antoine Dupanloup of Orleáns, Friedrich Joseph Von Schwarzenberg of Prague, Joseph Othmar von Rauscher of Vienna, and some 150 followers. We might recall that this doctrine was not known in the early Church. As late as the beginning of the nineteenth century the general belief was that the Church's infallibility was exercised by the pope in conjunction with a general council. In the United States, except for Miege and a dozen or so like him, most of the bishops opposed the definition. Some objected on theological grounds, while the majority seemed to have felt that it would be most inopportune. This difference of opinion was much the same throughout the Church.[12] France is a good example of how some bishops feared the reaction that would be aroused back home if the doctrine were to be formally defined. Ever since the famed Articles of 1682 defined the Gallican position, it was held there that a General Council is above the pope, that is, the pope must not interfere directly or indirectly in civil and temporal affairs. Moreover, in France the exercise of apostolic power was regulated by the laws and customs of the Gallican church as well as by the canons of the church.[13] While Gallicanism was no longer as critical an issue as it was in the seventeenth and eighteenth centuries, there were enough "state lawyers and jurisconsults" left to cause the Church considerable trouble in the event of a definition.[14]

The following excerpts from his letters show that Bishop Miege was quite aware of what was going on behind the scenes. On January 30, 1870, he wrote to Canon Alliaudi:

As you tell it in your good letter, the poor Gratry[15] only wiped out himself and his party; the explosion of his bomb has done more to alarm the Gallicans than the Ultramontanists. However, some of these Gentlemen praise the author and his work; I can hardly believe their sincerity. Finally, Mgr. D. . . [Dupanloup?] was successful in getting a promise from the three Portuguese bishops not to sign the petition for infallibility. After having read Gratry, these bishops went to see Mgr. D . . . and asked him what he thought of this brochure; this one approved it in a very pronounced manner, and these left him abruptly telling him that they were going to sign the petition that they had promised not to sign. It is thus that good work is done and continues to be done. If the Holy Father lives, and if the Council is able to continue its work, in spite of the intrigues and underhand dealings of certain spirits, the personal infallibility of the Pope—*positis ponendis*—will be defined, declared and proclaimed for the good of the chil-

dren of the Church, and for the good as well of their enemies. This at least is my hope and conviction.[16]

Bishop Miege believed that the Germans and Hungarians
were to be more feared than the Gallicans. And while his
"dear Americans" were siding with the Gallicans and the
Germans, he felt that when the time came most of them
would vote for papal infallibility.

On April 20, 1870, Bishop Miege again wrote to Canon
Alliaudi. He began with a very delicate reprimand to his
friend for printing his last letter in the *l'Echo des Alpes*. Then,
typically, he blamed his own "clumsiness" for not being clear
enough in pointing out that the letters were not meant for
publication. In the same letter he stated that brochures for
and against infallibility "continue to thwart one another."
Referring to a tract by Bishop Wilhelm Emmanuel von Ketteler
of Mainz, he added: "It is painful to see a man so zealous,
devout and edifying, take the road of the opposition; I am still
hoping that he will yield in good time. He has only the half of
his nose left to him; he lost the other part in a duel he had
while a colonel in a Prussian regiment. He gives me the
impression of a man who would not like someone to take the
little that remains to him."[17]

The chapter on papal infallibility was brought to a vote on
July 18, 1870. The previous day Bishop Dupanloup and his
supporters left Rome. With two exceptions, the 533 remaining
Fathers gave their *placet* ("it pleases"). With the exception of
Ignatius Dollinger and his supporters, bishops throughout the
world accepted the decision "as true and inspired."[18] Actually,
in its final form, the dogma did not mean that the pope could
now tell "infallible jokes" but simply that "when the Roman
Pontiff speaks *ex cathedra,* that is, when in the discharge of
his office as Doctor and Pastor of all Christians, in virtue of
his supreme Apostolic authority, he defines a doctrine concerning faith or morals to be held by the whole Church, he
enjoys, by the divine assistance promised him in Blessed
Peter, that infallibility with which the divine Redeemer willed
that His Church would be endowed for the purpose of defining doctrine concerning faith or morals, and therefore such
definitions of the Roman Pontiff are irreformable of themselves and not from the consent of the Church."[19]

On July 19, 1870, the Franco-Prussian War erupted between France and Germany. Many of the bishops left Rome immediately; those who remained worked until September 20 when the Italian army entered Rome. A month later Pius IX suspended the Council indefinitely.[20]

After the suspension of the Council, Bishop Miege remained in Rome for a few weeks to take care of several affairs pertaining to his vicariate. He then returned to Chevron to pay what would be his final farewell to the family, and especially to his beloved brother Urban, whom he would never see again. He next traveled to Ireland, birthplace of a large number of Catholics who had come to find in Kansas the bread and religious freedom they were unable to obtain in their native land. The Irish Catholics—particularly numerous in Leavenworth—were very grateful to their vicar apostolic, who had the careful consideration to visit their country before returning to America. They were especially happy to welcome several Irish priests, who were to be charged with caring for their spiritual needs.[21]

On his return Bishop Miege was greeted with raptures of joy throughout his vicariate, but especially in Leavenworth. He wrote to his brother Urban telling him all about the festivities, but unfortunately the letter never arrived. An excellent report of the reception was printed by the Leavenworth *Monitor.* We rely on it here, together with a lead article in the *Leavenworth Daily Times,* for our information.

On Sunday morning, November 20, 1870, a solemn pontifical high Mass was celebrated by Bishop Miege. He was assisted by Fathers Corbett, Parker, and Favre, as assistant priest, subdeacon, and master of ceremonies, respectively. Father Thomas Butler, we are told, preached an excellent sermon. Mozart's *Twelfth Mass* was beautifully sung to the accompaniment of the organ and a fine orchestra "with unusually imposing effect." That afternoon at three P.M. "a large procession consisting of various Catholic societies formed at the German Church on Broadway and, headed by the Fort Band, marched down that street to Delaware, down Delaware to Fifth, and up Fifth to the Bishop's residence, where an immense crowd of people, besides those who marched in the procession, were already gathered." John Beringer, a parishioner, represented his fellows in reading an address of welcome. He expressed "the pleasure which they felt in the safe return of their beloved Bishop, whose devotion to both church and people had endeared him to all." The address further lauded him for his support of the pope on the issue of infallibility. When Beringer had finished, the bishop thanked everyone for the honor they did him in so great a welcome. He complimented the benevolent societies for the good they had been doing and expressed the hope that they would continue to prosper. The bishop spoke in so low a voice that it was difficult to hear him from a distance. The *Times* called the occasion "one of great interest among the Catholics, who hold Bishop Miege in very high esteem." The *Monitor* mentioned the "grandiose character of this reception, the special interest shown by everyone." It was altogether "a striking testimony to the worth of the man, and of the great esteem which he enjoys among his diocesans."[22]

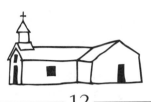

12

THE SOUTH AMERICAN EXPERIENCE

On his return from the Vatican Council, Bishop Miege made it his principal preoccupation to find means to cover the debts he had contracted in constructing the cathedral as well as the several schools and charitable institutions he had provided for his people. The trouble was that, with the rapid construction of the railroads after the Civil War, some Missouri River towns began to decline. Once the Kansas Pacific later the Union Pacific—was constructed westward from Kansas City, Leavenworth no longer could become the metropolis it was once envisioned. The Catholic population of the town dwindled, and "the Sunday collection of the Cathedral declined by half."[1] The plans the bishop had made to persuade his clergy to help him solve the debt were not successful. As he told his brother, the priests pretended to know that, if he paid his debts, he would renounce Kansas. Consequently, they showed little interest in the success of the enterprise. He added: "It is a pretext for some of them; it is not easy to collect and they fear the need."[2] At the same time both Propaganda and the Father General informed him that they would not accept his resignation until he had paid most of his debts.

There seems to have been a bit of a misunderstanding on the bishop's part in this matter. In July 1871, Father Beckx wrote to Miege congratulating him on having obtained a coadjutor, "a man religious, prudent, pious, full of apostolic zeal, knowing the country. . . ." He expressed the hope that between them they would devise means "for gradually taking care of the necessities" that rendered him so anxious. The Father General then added: "But I do not think it advisable for you to leave your place until the debts have been paid or at least until it is so arranged that they will not seem be a burden upon your successor. . . ."[3]

Apparently Bishop Miege took the letter to be more demanding than was intended. The following November Father Beckx wrote a second letter. We cite it here in part because, in addition to clarifying his position, it shows why the Society of Jesus had to be so careful in such matters:

> The letter of your illustrious reverence which I recently received, edified me on the one hand, but on the other pained me. I gladly perceived in it how little transient dignities and honors are enjoyed by you, rather how by every effort and desire you seek to give them up. However, I was hurt that my last letter to you caused you pain. But if you consider more attentively the letter of July 23, you will see that it is not to be interpreted in a more severe sense than it presents itself. For your honor and that of the Society I indicated that it was not exactly necessary that all debts be paid off, but that your affairs be so arranged that they do not seem to burden your successor. This will be accomplished if your reverence made a contract by which you hand over to your successor Church and residence and anything else with their support, and at the same time what can bring income, e.g., farms, by which debts can be paid off, etc., so that your successor accept these and so free you and the Society from any obligation. This instrument should be prepared in two copies, by which, first, this transfer be accomplished actively and passively, and, second, it be declared by your successor that he freely accept this transfer and that he is satisfied by it, and that he takes on himself the payment of any unpaid debts.
>
> If such a contract established by both parties is signed and each party has a copy, I see no difficulty hindering you from giving up the Vicariate as you desire. And be

assured . . . I desire with you that you be freed from it as soon as possible. We should demand the document I referred to above lest afterwards we be accused of leaving so many thousand debts and of having brought harm to the Mission.[4]

As a result of this "magnificent situation," as the bishop called it, he became determined to visit South America at the invitation of one or other of his bishop-friends. He would thus try the liberality and charity of the people of South America to raise funds. He felt that he would be successful if the good Lord gave him the necessary strength and courage. And while it would be a heavy burden "for an old machine all full of rhumatism," he concluded with the old proverb that: "The sky is in the South as well as in the North."[5]

Another factor that helped convince Bishop Miege to take the then dangerous journey south was the appointment, in June 1871, of Bishop Louis Mary Fink, O.S.B., as his coadjutor. Miege knew he would be leaving his diocese in capable hands. Before departing for Rome to attend the Vatican Council, Bishop Miege had appointed Fink, then prior of the Benedictines in Atchison, Kansas, administrator of the vicariate during his absence. He had a very high regard for him. While he would have preferred Rome accept his resignation, he was pleased when Prior Louis was appointed his coadjutor. At the time of his consecration in Chicago, the new bishop was in such poor health that Bishop Foley, his consecrator, reportedly remarked that it was a waste of holy oil.[6] A month later Bishop Miege told his brother: "I finally have a coadjutor! He is a worthy man fearing God and the devil, and serving the good Master with all the generosity of a true son of Saint Benedict. He is almost six feet tall, with a foot and a half beard, but thin as a rail."[7] As coadjutor and then as Miege's successor, Bishop Fink served Leavenworth well until his death at seventy on March 17, 1904.

Bishop Miege departed from Leavenworth on Thursday, October 12, 1871. He took the Kansas Pacific to Denver, where he spent a day or two with his successor, Bishop Joseph Machebeuf. He then headed for San Francisco, arriving on Saturday, October 21. Two days later, in a letter to his brother, he gave an interesting account of his forty-eight hour train ride over the mountains:

There was a bit of snow in the mountains, a grand fire going in the cars, a good table and good cots, all went well as possible. But what a frightful defile we passed! In many places the railroad is cut into the rock on the side of tremendous precipices. From the cars we could see the precipice up to 1,200 feet in depth, from which we were separated by only 3 to 4 feet, without barrier and without protection, when the slightest accident would hurl everything into the abyss without leaving a trace. I thought of the good guardian angels and asked them to help us cross these terrible mountains without accident. Our Americans do not like delays, and provided that they have a route, they are content. Four or five hundred persons will be killed one of these days; then public opinion will demand tunnels and they will supply them. There are now thirteen places on this road which have a covering, built by the railroad company, to prevent the snow from accumulating in the defiles. These coverings cost them 1,200,000 francs per league. There are a lot of bad passes in the Rocky Mountains, but they are not particularly extraordinary for a Savoyard. Everything I am telling you takes place in the Sierra Nevada, which one crosses before arriving at San Francisco.[8]

After the Jesuits were driven out of Italy in 1848, a considerable number from the Piedmont province were assigned to work in California and Oregon. It is not surprising, then, that Bishop Miege should have met many of his old friends, who received him with both kindness and charity. They had a splendid college at San Francisco and a fine boarding school at Santa Clara.[9]

The bishop waxed eloquently on the merits of California, famed for its fruits and its vines. He claimed to have seen "truly magnificent" pears that weighed from four to six pounds. He explained to his brother how the Jesuits there were making what they called "old wine":

They put red wine in a container at 140 degrees Fahrenheit—it is the thermometer of our country—and after having allowed it sufficiently long time to extract certain gasses, they let it cool and put it in bottles. This is a

French invention, and perhaps our good Curé knows of it. The red wine becomes the color of his Fontainebleau; it is strong and very delightful to the taste; one would actually take it for wine of eight to ten years.[10]

In spite of his fatigue and occasional serious bouts with illness, Bishop Miege faithfully wrote to his brother. Good and bad things always happened to him. The fact, too, that he possessed fine powers of observation added all the more interest to his letters. These letters, together with correspondence written to friends in the States, is our source of information for the bishop's travels in South America.

Bishop Miege left San Francisco aboard an American steamer at eleven A.M. on Friday, November 3, 1871. An elderly Spanish-speaking Jesuit, who had been south on two previous occasions, served as his companion. They planned to go first to Panama, where they would leave the American ship and board an English steamer for Guayaquil, Ecuador. It was the bishop of Guayaquil, a fellow Jesuit, who had assured Miege that he could collect enough to pay his debts by coming to South America. The journey from Panama to the Ecuadorian seacoast town took fifteen days. Since the bishop's letters that were written in the early months of 1872 are missing, we know nothing of the voyage down nor of the success or failure of his stay in Guayaquil.

Bishop Miege's first extant letter from South America to his brother was written from Santiago, Chile, on November 4, 1872. He referred to Santiago as a "lovely city of 160,000 souls, situated in a plain at the foot of the Cordilleras." Due to the frequent and violent earthquakes that wracked the area, the city's houses were mostly two stories high. "Everything has an air of progress, of cleanliness and of elegance, which has nowhere impressed me such as here," wrote the bishop. He then went on to explain to his brother how the seasons of Chile differed so from those of his native Savoy. November, the most beautiful month of the year and richest in flowers, was consecrated to the Blessed Mother. The heat of summer, said to be very severe, was felt in December, January, and February. "However," he added, "the great advantage of this country is that the nights are cool all year long; a good coverlet is welcome even in the summer; a person can sleep and rest from the fatigues of the journey and begin with sufficient courage the pace of the previous day."[11]

When Bishop Miege wrote in 1872, society in Santiago was still composed of three distinct classes—the aristocracy, the commercial elite, and the working class. The first possessed the land and controlled the labor. It was comprised of the old nobility: dukes, marquis, counts, and viscounts. However, the bishop remarked, "the titles have disappeared with the royalty; but the good breeding, the manners, the spirit of faith, of charity, of religion remain with a certain air of patriarchal nobility that is singularly pleasing and attractive."[12] A bit of the bishop's European background seems to have crept in here.

If Bishop Miege was a bit on the snobbish side in his praise of the upper class, American influence emerged in the following anecdote relayed to his brother. After praising the clergy for their learning and for the respect and influence they wielded in the community, he described an association of some 150 young folks who were "a strong resource against evil" in Santiago. The society was made up of barristers, deputies, writers, and independent gentlemen—in large part, students or former students of the city's Jesuit college. The bishop continues the story:

> One of them, a young man twenty-seven years old . . . was recently an actor in a scene which made a lot of noise in the whole of Chile. He is a deputy and secretary of the Chamber. A red deputy in a speech allowed himself to attack the Sisters of Charity. Our young Catholic, enraged, interrupted him with words which are not in all the dictionaries, and the other, even more angered, heaped on him all the insults he could think of. This ended the assembly. When the deputies left the Chamber, our young man placed himself at the door and when the red came out, he told him to get ready to receive the punishment his impudence merited. The other, who carried a large cane, raised it on the head of his adversary; but a punch directed in time between the two eyes sent the individual and his cane rolling on the pavement. He got up again, swearing like a Cossack and returned to the attack, but to receive in the same place a mark which still has not been erased. Then friends

intervened and the scene was finished except for the usage received.[13]

The bishop did not think this was very nice, but he did think it had a humorous side.

Unfortunately, conditions were deplorable in Santiago as well as the port city of Valparaíso at the time of the bishop's visit. Both cities were decimated by a smallpox epidemic, and public charity was directed toward relief of the victims.[14] Moreover, the Jesuit fathers in Santiago had just collected five hundred thousand francs for a new church they were building. Add to this the fact that a preacher of the foreign missions had left the city before Miege arrived. Still, he managed to collect some twenty-six thousand francs with promise of more. Consequently, he became determined to remain in Chile through February 1873 and only then depart for Montevideo, the capital city of Uruguay, in March.[15]

Bishop Miege was not idle during his stay in Santiago. In his November 1872 letter to his brother he mentioned that he had already confirmed twenty thousand persons in the archdiocese—and eleven thousand alone in Saint Philippe's parish—and that he expected to confirm twenty thousand more before departing. Confirmation in Santiago had not been publicly administered for fourteen years due to the age and infirmities of the city's venerable archbishop, who was seventy-six years old at the time.

On March 3, 1873, Bishop Miege left Chile for Argentina. He had a choice of two routes: by sea through the Strait of Magellan or by land over the Cordilleras. Though he preferred the first, the very thought of the storms of the South made him determined to choose the land route "on the principle that between two evils one must choose the lesser."[16] We are fortunate in his choice since we are left with minute details of the dangers of such travel in late nineteenth-century South America. The account of the passage over the mountains is given in a letter to his brother from Cordova dated April 8, 1873.

Bishop Miege departed from Valparaíso, a coastal town a few miles northwest of Santiago, begging our Lord, as he tells us, to bless the good people of Chile who seemed to him to be much superior to all he had seen thus far in his South

American travels. The railroad took him to San Philippe, then its terminal, where he stayed for a few days with his friend the Curé. Here he added to the eleven thousand confirmations he had administered previously. Here, too, he made his final preparations for travel. He was fortunate in finding a traveling companion, a Mercedaire father, who was returning to his convent at Mendoza. Between the two, they rented five mules and engaged two men to guide them and serve their needs. Three of the mules were used as pack animals. Mules were preferred to horses because they were more surefooted.[17]

Two short stages of seventy-five miles brought the party to the foot of the Cordilleras by a "gently sloping road and generally in fairly good condition." At six o'clock in the evening on the second day, they arrived at a small house situated at the foot of the mountain. There they were offered two beds on the ground in a roofless room. That night a snowstorm roared on the mountain and threatened to invade the "episcopal palace." They got a "good fright" but, in spite of the storm, they were on their way the next morning by five o'clock ready for the ascent.[18] The reason for the early start was that the summit of the mountain had to be passed before eleven o'clock in the morning in order to avoid the dangerous gusts of wind. By ten-thirty, after climbing fourteen thousand feet "as perpendicular as a mule could do them . . . ," they arrived at the highest point in the road. The road was bordered on both sides by a sharply inclined plain of four to five hundred feet, a precipice so steep that, if one fell, it would guarantee instant death. What remained of traveler and his mount, the bishop remarked, would not be worth "all the silk robes of Jason's wife."[19]

At this point, the bishop's narrative is not too clear. Apparently the ascent was done in two stages, since he mentions encountering snow halfway up and meeting a family who provided them with good services. The place where they did stop was not the best furnished, but the good couple gave the bishop and his companion their own mattresses. They made a meal of bread, salted meat, and wine.[20]

Arriving at the top of the pass, the party rested for a quarter of an hour and then began the descent. While this stage of the trip was less difficult, it was much more fatiguing. One reason was that, unlike contemporary western saddles,

saddles at that time had no pommel. Hence, there was always the danger of falling over the head of the mule. To avoid such an occurrence one had to sit erect and lean back during the sharp descents—extremely tiresome for a person weighing 250 or more pounds. The bishop and his fellows survived the highest point in good order. However, there still remained another four days of Cordilleras, along a pass featuring some very difficult maneuvering. The bishop explained:

> One of these passes which is called *Lhallier,* is so difficult that one does it only on foot. Burdened mules often tumble down to the bottom, where their masters usually succeed in stopping them, and thus prevent them from falling over a frightful precipice, situated a few steps away. A bit farther on we encountered the most difficult step of the whole journey: a perpendicular crag. To its left is a road so narrow that only one mule could pass by at a time, and at the right a precipice of 1,000 to 1,500 feet. I confess that in going by there I felt quite giddy; I closed my eyes and gave our Blessed Mother the care of her poor child. All went well. But a convoy of loaded mules which preceded us was not as fortunate. One of them fell, and trying to get up, placed a foot beyond the road. It tumbled over the precipice and we saw nothing of it any more. . . . We saw on this occasion a large number of condors that hovered above the victim; for when they are hungry they attack everything they encounter and kill whatever they can. They are so large that spread wings extend up to 15 feet. Food is never lacking for them in the spring, summer and fall seasons when thousands of cattle, cows, horses and mules cross these mountains for Chile and Peru. Indeed the roads are covered with carcasses of these animals, which could no longer move along. Since they found nothing to eat except thorn bushes, they did not delay dying and being devoured.[21]

Finally, after seven days the bishop arrived at Mendoza, where he stayed with the Fathers of Mercy, who received him with great kindness. Somehow they knew the day of his arrival and sent out two carriages to meet him about fifteen miles from town. Little wonder that he and his companion uttered a cry of joy when they saw the carriages.

It took but two days of rest to regain their strength. One wonders at the charity of the people of this small village who, in a matter of two days, gave the bishop twelve hundred francs. This was all the more remarkable since thirteen years before an earthquake completely leveled the place, crushing to death eight thousand of its fourteen thousand inhabitants. A convent of sisters, who ran a large boarding school for girls, lost eighteen sisters and twenty-eight boarders. Still, the town had its good points. It was surrounded by extremely rich and fertile lands, which produced grain in abundance and the best fruits in South America. A bit east of Mendoza began the great plains, which stretched all the way to Buenos Aires, and which, added the bishop, "are ravaged by savages and brigands who kill and rob all the isolated families who establish themselves there."[22]

After eight days of rest and a few hundred confirmations, Bishop Miege left Mendoza by stagecoach for Cordova, some 390 miles to the northeast. As the crow flies the distance was not great, but at that time the stage route would probably have extended far into the plains. A letter written by Bishop Miege from Cordova in April 1873, provides some interesting information on travel by coach in South America during that time:

The coach could hold 9 persons; it was full. I took a seat on the outside with the driver to whom I was especially recommended and who treated me perfectly well during the whole voyage. I had the advantage of seeing everything, of enjoying the breeze and leaning upon a crossbar. All that was not a little matter in a voyage of eight days. The coach was drawn by ten horses mounted by ten postilions, the most skilful horsemen I have ever encountered. Just imagine two horses to a pole, then a strong line of cowhide seventy feet long, from which go five smaller lines from each side with an iron clasp, which is attached to the saddle of the postilion. We departed in a full gallop, and it is gallop every day and every instant throughout the course of the voyage. The cries of the postilions are also unceasing as the lashes of the whips, and after a quarter of an hour these poor animals are covered with blood and sweat. Happily the relays are at two and a half leagues, three leagues at most, and this is all the horses can take without dying in their trappings. In this way we made from 75 to 80 miles each day.[23]

A stop was made each night. The procedure demanded that, on arrival, two sheep be bought, skinned, cut in two parts, and placed on a fire, where they were grilled to perfection. Since knives and forks were not the custom in the plains of Argentina, each one would take a piece according to individual capacity. Apparently, the remnants were never of much account. That first night a frightful rain and hailstorm threatened to deluge the group. The downpour was so great that the next morning they "galloped for half the trip in three feet of water."[24] All went well enough until they came to the Rio Quinto. The driver sent one of the postilions to see if a crossing were possible. Bishop Miege continues the story:

> All the travelers, with the exception of a nice old lady and me, crossed over on horseback, and the coach entered the river; but after a few steps a horse entangled himself in his line and was almost drowned; the current carried him rolling for a good distance; fortunately a large boulder stopped him and set him on his feet. Since we were near the relay it was soon replaced, but after a few steps more a new delay. They sent for four more horses, and in spite of the shouts and the whippings, everything was useless; there we were bogged down between huge rocks which there was no hope of passing. During all this time the good old lady wept, making signs of the cross, making promises to Saint Anthony, and demanding that I bless the river. Finally the men were obliged to turn to the wheels, and after five hours passed in a dangerous situation, we had the consolation of reaching the opposite bank.[25]

After all the excitement it was unanimously decided to call it a day. Supper was made, and the party prepared to retire. But suddenly the commanding officer of a nearby military station dashed up "at full gallop" to inform the group that a band

of brigands was two leagues away and would attack during
the night. What followed sounds like a three-reel comedy. On
hand were two carbines and a revolver. Everything was made
ready for battle. There even was an advance guard—carrying
beds "for fear of losing their night's sleep." Before retiring
they discharged the two carbines to see if they worked. They
recharged them, and everybody cautiously tried to sleep.
Fortunately the night was "as tranquil as all the others," and at
five o'clock in the morning the party was on its daily way
"galloping and getting tired."[26]

At Villa Maria, a village southwest of Cordova, Bishop
Miege took the train and, after three hours, arrived at his destination. Here again he was received with great kindness by
his Jesuit brethren. He explained to his brother that Cordova
was a town of thirty thousand inhabitants. It was renowned
for its university, the piety of its people, and the almost
monastic silence that prevailed day and night in its streets.[27]

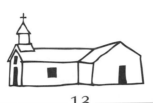

— 13 —
BRAZIL AND THE VOYAGE NORTH

Bishop Miege left Montevideo, Uruguay, on October 17, 1872, and after "four days of seasickness," arrived at Rio de Janeiro at two o'clock in the afternoon on October 21. Four days seem like a long time to complete the thousand-mile trip up the coast. The bishop does not tell us what sort of vessel he took. If it was an ordinary coastal steamer, it would likely have visited several ports along the way. Moreover, the southerly flowing Brazil currents and somewhat adverse winds at that season may have helped impede the progress of the little ship. After spending most of the four days in bed, the bishop was happy to disembark "immediately" on arriving at Rio, where he made his way to the convent of the Capuchins with whom he was to stay.

The Capuchin Fathers and brothers lived at the top of a very steep hill, and Bishop Miege had to make the climb "under a burning sun, at an hour when it makes itself felt stronger than ever." He tells us that, clad in winter apparel and covered with sweat, he "breathed out like a steam engine."[1] Why he made the climb on foot, weak and fatigued as he was, is a mystery. However, two days of rest just about "repaired the breaches." Immediately, he began to prepare a list of prominent Brazilians and then sent a circular in Portuguese to their attention. The bishop explained his plan to his brother:

If they send their alms, very well! If not, I will have to
visit them and speak to them about my problem.
Sometimes they speak neither English, or French, or
Spanish, or Italian; and I, though I more or less understand Portuguese, am still not able to speak it. Just imagine what sort of figure I must make to these marquis,
dukes, counts and barons.[2]

Soon after arriving in Rio, Bishop Miege visited the apostolic nuncio, who received him very well. He then paid his
respects to the bishop whom he found to be "extremely amiable" and "possessed of an openness and sincerity that is truly
charming." The bishop gave him a pamphlet against
Freemasonry that he had written and printed; he added a
donation of 150,000 Brazilian reis, or 375 francs.

About the same time, Bishop Miege visited an elderly
Englishman, who loved the Jesuits and helped them with his
generous benefactions. While apparently enjoying life, he
delighted in spending his immense fortune in charitable
deeds. "His entire happiness," the bishop wrote, "consists in
serving God and doing good to his neighbor. He had the
goodness to give me 500,000 reis, or 1,250 francs."

The old gentleman, whose name was not given, accompanied Bishop Miege to the residence of the emperor, Don
Pedro II. However, for some mysterious reason, while
esteemed by the emperor, he did not want to be seen by
him.[3] The bishop had a few problems of his own. He mentioned to his brother that, if the good emperor came to
know that he was a Jesuit, his reception would have been
more than cold. Apparently, the monarch had been convinced that the Jesuits were a threat to the peace of govern-
ments in general by virtue of their alleged plots and
underhand dealings. "The poor Jesuits," added Miege. "May
the good God bless them and help them."[4] However, the
bishop was actually well received by the emperor, who
wanted to know all about the Indian missions of Kansas.
After being told of the missions' needs, he responded with a
gift of one thousand francs.

Bishop Miege's description of Rio de Janeiro in the late
1800s is worth mentioning. He wrote:

The port of Rio de Janeiro, they say, is the most beautiful in the world; it is certainly the most beautiful that I have seen; it is ten leagues in circumference and can hold the largest ships. It is defended by three forts at the entrance of the roadstead, and still another on the inside, almost in front of the principal part of the city. To give you an idea of Rio de Janeiro, you have to imagine beautiful hills standing against low mountains. Between the different hills there are quite narrow valleys; these valleys and the space that separates the hills from the sea form the commercial section of the city. The heights are occupied by convents, churches, residences of the nobles and wealthy merchants. It is a very beautiful city. Almost the entire circumference of the roadstead is inhabited; and at night the effect of this immense illumination with gas, whose lights are reflected in the waters of the bay, certainly affords a magnificent spectacle from the top of these beautiful hills that command a view of the entire perspective.[5]

On December 3, 1873, after his morning mass, Bishop Miege was seized with a severe attack of yellow fever. He had been running about the streets of Rio and, considering his age, his weight, his run-down condition, and the severe heat, the illness was almost to be expected. Fortunately, the malady was caught in time. The aid of a good doctor, together with the care of the Lazarist Fathers, soon got him back on his feet, though in a very enfeebled condition. When his doctor ordered a change of climate, he set out for Santos by ship and then to São Paulo by rail. Actually this did not represent too great a change in his plans since, as early as March 1873, he had been considering such a trip. An added incentive was the existence of a convent of Capuchins from Savoy and a convent of Sisters of Saint Joseph from Chambéry. A few miles away was a large Jesuit college, where he could find some of his old friends from Rome days.

Arriving in São Paulo, Bishop Miege went straight to the major seminary, which was run by the Capuchin Fathers—all from Savoy. Most of them had been to Conflans, Chevron, and La Forêt and were acquainted with Urban Miege and many of his friends. The bishop spoke of this meeting as "the finest moment" of his voyage. He stayed with his Capuchin friends until the day after Christmas. He then took the train for Itu, normally a five-hour run but extended to nine-and-a-half hours because of a derailment.[6]

At the time of the bishop's visit, the Jesuits at Itu were building a large college. Miege did not think it would ever be completed "because of the opposition and propaganda of the secret societies" against the Society. He noted that the Fathers were not tolerated, and that the laws of the Marquis de Pombal still prevailed against them; that is, the government could, at a moment's notice, order them to pack up and leave. Buildings, which had been erected at enormous cost, could then be taken over by the authorities. Still, Brazil continued to be full of colleges, churches, and other memorials to the "Old Society"—that is, prior to the Society's expulsion—and the new college would add to the number.[7]

For a better understanding of Bishop Miege's letters, it may be worthwhile to digress for a moment and explain the situation that arose in Brazil from the grand mixture of Freemasonry and Catholicism. Freemasonry, it will be recalled, stemmed from the medieval English craft guilds of stonemasons. As time passed, more and more honorary members were admitted to the lodges, ostensibly to bolster their sagging membership. During the eighteenth century, when the philosophy of the Enlightenment—deistic, materialistic, rationalistic—became so popular, many of its tenets crept into the thinking of the masonic lodges. There was no thought of denying the existence of God, but God as the Grand Architect of the Universe was not a personal God. Such beliefs as the Trinity, miracles, or inspiration of the Scriptures in the traditional sense were discarded as being contrary to reason. However, in the course of the nineteenth century, more of the traditional Christian observances were reinstated. Significantly, one did not have to be a Christian in order to be a mason. Basically, Freemasonry has been an English institution stemming from the formation of the Grand Lodge of England. Today its worldwide membership is overwhelmingly English-speaking. Possibly the reason for its conservatism has been that it draws its membership largely from the Protestant churches of the United Kingdom and North America.

Over the years the Catholic Church has condemned Freemasonry for its "naturalism, demand for oaths," and "religious indifferentism."[8] Many Protestant churches, among them Lutheran, Quakers, Mennonites, Jehovah's Witnesses, Mormons, Wesleyans, and others, have on occasion issued prohibitions for its members. Often, however, such prohibitions did not contain sufficient authority. Moreover, Christians, including Catholics, frequently lacked a basic understanding of Freemasonry in general. This brings us to the situation in South America and, specifically, Brazil.

Bishop Miege pointed out to his brother:

Brazil is a country of innumerable confraternities, and many processions; it is also a land of very little religious instruction, and still less of religious practice. Under the title of beneficence, Masonry has succeeded in coming up with many experts who introduce themselves into the said confraternities, practically all of which are governed by it; and meanwhile these fine gentlemen after having spent the evening at the lodge, march the next day in procession as penitents clad in white, allowing themselves the most horrible blasphemies against the Immaculate Conception, against the infallibility of the Pope and against everything that displeases them.[9]

The trouble was that papal documents condemning Freemasonry were never published in Brazil. As a result, it was commonly thought that Brazilian masonry was different from masonry in general and that even the clergy could join if they so wished. An uproar ensued when the bishops, generally good and strong, determined to put an end to the abuses and proclaimed that Freemasonry in Brazil was no better than that of other countries. A crisis followed. Since Bishop Miege was in Brazil when it occurred, we will let him tell the story:

The Bishop of Pernambuco gave orders to the confraternities to expel the Freemasons under pain of interdict for their chapels; they refused; he interdicted them. You figure out the fury and grinding of teeth! . . . The affair has been brought to Congress, and the President of the Council of Ministers, who is Grand-Orient, pleaded the cause of the Freemasons. The Congress, almost entirely made up of this sect, decided that the Bishop should annul his order or he would be brought before the courts. The Bishop, well informed, refused to withdraw his order and declared the court incompetent. Then the Government accused him of obeying a foreign power, the Pope, against the constitution of the Empire. This is the point on which he will have to defend himself, but recognizing the competence of the tribunal he will not defend himself. The penalty of the offense is from four to six years in prison. The actual cause of the accusation comes to this, that the Bishop published a letter of the Holy Father against Brazilian freemasonry without the permission of the government.[10]

Finally, a battleship arrived and the bishop of Pernambuco was taken to Rio.

Bishop Miege remained with his Jesuit brethren at Itu for a month and a half and then returned to Rio. While there he assisted together with the bishop of Rio, at the trial of the bishop of Pernambuco. In a later letter to his brother he mentioned how the bishop was condemned to four years of hard labor for not lifting the interdict issued against the chapels under the control of the Freemasons. The emperor commuted the penalty to four years confinement in a fortress of the port. Bishop Miege added: "There are in this entire affair details so revolting with iniquities, such a prostitution of justice and equity, that we cannot help from trembling for a country where the Government itself is the promoter and executor of such shocking injustices."[11]

On February 24, Bishop Miege boarded the United States steamer *Merrymack* bound for New York. He described the *Merrymack* as a large ship with screw propellers and well-aired rooms. All the crew were Irish except for the three first officers and the engineers. On this trip, Bishop Miege was accompanied by his dear friend the Abbé Goud, who planned to visit Kansas with him. Four days of rough seas and illness brought the bishop to the magnificent bay of Bahia, Brazil. There he visited the upper town. As he explained to his brother:

They mount it by elevators. One makes use of these latter when one wants to do in five minutes and without fatigue, what one could only do in three quarters of an hour by a very fatiguing and very difficult climb. We took the shortest way and the shortest way is the easiest. With paying five solds [sols] we were on the hill.[12]

After visiting at the home of the Lazarists and the Sisters of Charity, the bishop and his companion returned to the ship "all bathed in sweat and very tired." Bishop Miege did not particularly like Bahia, which he described as beautiful from a distance but otherwise terribly dirty.

Two days later the *Merrymack* docked at Pernambuco, but since the layover was only six hours, the bishop did not go ashore. The journey from Pernambuco to Pará, a distance of about sixteen hundred miles, usually took six or seven days. But again Bishop Miege proved to be somewhat of a Jonah. He describes the situation:

After thirty hours of good travel, towards the early hours of the night we heard a tremendous disturbance in the bottom of the ship, which caused us to fear a rock or the bursting of the engine. Happily it was this latter hypothesis that was verified. The large iron beam fourteen inches in diameter, which turned the screw propeller, crashed and the part convex with the steam engine struck the bottom of the boat with such force that, had it been less robust, a gap would have opened. But fortunately the engine was able to get loose before any damage could occur. We were reduced to sails to move a boat that carried 18,000 sacks of coffee.[13]

At the mercy of the winds, it took the ship fourteen days to reach the capital city of Belém, which was well up the Amazon River.

During the ten days it took to repair the machinery, Bishop Miege visited Bishop Masedo of Pará, whom he had met at the Council. He and the Abbé were received with the greatest goodwill and charity. After returning to the States, he received a letter from Bishop Masedo, who was then in prison for the same reason as his predecessor, Bishop Olinda. Bishop Miege described him as "the best theologian, the best canonist, and the best man of letters in Brazil." Apparently, the government feared him because of the authority and respect he elicited from the people of distant Pará, which was far from the seat of power.[14]

The journey northward was resumed on March 22. When the *Merrymack* arrived "hobbling along" at Saint Thomas in the Virgin Islands on April 30, the bishop bade adieu to that unfortunate ship. A few days later he departed for Puerto Rico, arriving at five o'clock the next morning. He went straight to the Jesuit college, where he had the happiness of meeting an old fellow prefect from Chambéry days. He stayed eight days in Puerto Rico, managing at the same time to gather enough funds to return to Kansas.[15]

The next step took Bishop Miege to Havana, where he arrived on April 18. The Jesuits had a large college there and, with their influence, he hoped to reduce still more the remaining 250,000 francs of his debt. However, in spite of his pleading, he was able to collect only two thousand francs. He had a few interesting comments to make on the political situation in Cuba, however. He noted that the Spanish government gave the college to the Jesuits, thinking them sufficiently patriotic to counterbalance the revolutionary ideas of the colonists. At the same time, they drove the Jesuits out of Spain because they feared too much patriotism there. He thought that the revolution had ruined Cuba both morally and financially.[16]

After three weeks in Havana a very stormy sea carried the bishop and his companion to New Orleans. Though the storm lasted fully three days, there was always the consolation of finally returning to the United States. The Fathers of the Jesuit Province of Lyons, Miege's home province, were centered in New Orleans, where they had a day school (the present Loyola University) and a lovely church. In Mobile, Alabama, they operated a large boarding school (the present Spring Hill College). They also maintained a residence in Georgia. Bishop Miege visited his old companions, some of whom he had not seen for more than thirty years. Among them was Father Curioz, with whom he had been a prefect at the college in Milan and later a student at the Roman College. At Mobile he found Father Usannay, whom he last saw during their novitiate days some thirty-seven years before. The bishop commented about the latter:

He is exactly the same man, and his nose has not at all lost its formidable dimensions. He is an excellent religious, who renders genuine services to the mission.[17]

A thirty-three hour railroad trip and much fatigue brought the bishop to St. Louis on May 20. After a brief visit with the father provincial, together with his friend the Abbé Goud, he left for Leavenworth, arriving there on May 25, 1874. The long and difficult voyage, begun on October 12, 1871, had finally ended. The bishop added a heartfelt "Praise God and Mary!"

14

BISHOP MIEGE RETIRES

Announcing Bishop Miege's return to Leavenworth after his long stay in South America, the *Leavenworth Daily Times* noted: "A large number of citizens of both Catholic and Protestant belief, visited the Bishop yesterday, and greeted his return with expressions of good will and pleasure."[1] Bishop Miege also mentioned that between their visits and letters he had scarcely a moment to spare, "all spent in working from 6 o'clock in the morning to 11 o'clock in the evening."[2]

Though the South American venture was not a particularly great success, Bishop Miege did manage to raise about half the remaining debt on the cathedral, approximately $42,000. A fair was organized in Leavenworth to help collect additional funds. One of the most valuable articles to be raffled was a gold trophy cup given to the bishop in Argentina. An unidentified woman won it and presented it to the sisters at Saint Mary's Academy. At the time the sisters did not have a chalice of their own, so the cup was blessed and used as one.

On June 5, 1874, at the request of Bishop Miege, Bishop Louis Fink signed a document stating that the former had discharged a considerable part of the debt and that he, in turn, would make every effort to pay off the remainder.[3] Garin adds that while the bishop did not settle all debts, his superiors, taking into account the bishop's age and his immense efforts, finally granted him his freedom.[4]

In midsummer 1874, Bishop Miege "bravely stole away from Leavenworth" to make an eight-day retreat, which he had been forced to delay for four years. He hid himself for ten days of prayer and reflection at Saint Mary's of the Potawatomi, his old residence, where the Fathers had just built a fine college. Here he sincerely begged our Lord and his good Mother that it be his last retreat as a bishop. He added: "Mary always hears the poor who have recourse to her, and I trust that my request will be granted, if it is in the plans of God." He further assured his brother that, when the news arrived, he would immediately notify him.[5]

The bishop also mentioned to his brother that he had sent letters and documents to Fiesole, Italy, where the father general and his assistants were residing. After three months he had not received a reply, which was beginning to get on his nerves. Still, he had the grace to add: "But after all the good God, who wishes or permits these disappointments has without doubt his good reasons, and what remains for us to do, little boys (monkeys) that we are, is the *fiat voluntas tua* ['may your will be done']."[6] He also mentioned how seriously preoccupied he had been since his return, a preoccupation that fatigued him morally and physically and without any immediate hope of seeing the end.

In late November, Bishop Miege wrote to tell Urban that he might see him again soon. He had finally received his reply from Rome. The Roman authorities had asked for more information before accepting his resignation. He told Urban he thought all this delay to be a subterfuge to cause his affairs to drag out. He had given the requested information and was even willing to come to Rome, so persuaded was he that "an hour of conversation at Rome would be worth more than fifty letters written from Kansas." Although the prospect of another long sea voyage did not please him, twelve days of suffering were not too much to pay for the consolation of seeing the Holy Father and La Forêt again. He added: "It is peculiar with me that I have never been able to accustom myself to the Ocean. Indeed, in my voyage South I had 89 days on the two Oceans, and the last three days of sailing from Cuba to New Orleans struck me in such a fashion that I could not remain afoot for a single moment." He was not born to be a sailor, he concluded, and might as well reconcile himself to the fact.[7]

At the time of the bishop's letter in November, his coadjutor was in Pennsylvania gathering money to pay the twenty-one thousand francs needed to install a new furnace in the cathedral. The population of Leavenworth had declined by some nine thousand persons, many of them Catholic, in the previous five years, and thus the resources of the parish had diminished accordingly. Moreover, the legacy of the depression of 1873— its bank failures, foreclosings, and shutdown of countless factories and farms—was still evident in 1874. Add to this the drought and the grasshopper plague sweeping across Kansas at the same time, one sees why the bishop should have felt so dejected. As he told Urban, he was sometimes given to view everything in black. The struggles of the Church throughout the world also caused him considerable anguish—in Germany, Chile, and Brazil there was persecution; in France, feebleness and prostration; in Italy, misery and failure; and, at home, shocking iniquity and corruption. "One might almost say," he added, "that the time of the Apocalypse was not far away." The bishop concluded that when the Divine Providence wished to chastise Europeans, he sent them Napoleons, Bismarcks, Mazzinis, and Garibaldis; to the Americans, with their love for wealth, Providence sent droughts, grasshoppers, and financial panics.[8] Visiting his diocese that summer he found Kansas beautiful in the spring but burnt by the heat and devastated by the "vanguards of the Wrath of God."

The financial conditions imposed by Cardinal Giovanni Simeoni, Prefect of the Propaganda, and by Peter Beckx, father general of the Jesuits, before Bishop Miege could resign were finally considered as having been satisfied. On November 8, 1874, in an audience granted to the Prefect, Pius IX accepted Miege's resignation. Bishop Miege received the news of the acceptance, together with the following document, on December 11, 1874:

Since the Most Reverend Father John Baptist Miege, Bishop of Messenia in the lands of the infidels and Vicar Apostolic of the sovereign state of Kansas in the United States of North America, especially because of the precarious condition of his health under which he is laboring, has earnestly petitioned that he be permitted to relinquish the Apostolic Vicariate committed to his care, and since his request has been presented to our most Holy Father by Divine Providence Pius IX, in audience granted to the Secretary whose name appears below, on the 8th day of November, 1874, His Holiness kindly receiving the petition has deigned to accept the resignation offered by the most esteemed Reverend Father and Vicar Apostolic. Wherefore he ordered the present decree to be promulgated.

Given from the Quarters of the Sacred Congregation for the Propagation of the Faith the 18th day of November 1874, Alexander Cardinal Franchi, Prefect.

Joannes Simeoni, Secretary[9]

Bishop Miege wrote immediately to his coadjutor to inform him that his own resignation had been accepted and that he, in turn, had been named as his successor. He further announced that he would leave for St. Louis on December 14.

In a letter written on December 15 to his nephew Joseph-Eugene Miege, John Baptist stated that it was his intention, if he were permitted, to continue working in the United States, where there was a lot more good to be done. He added: "I sincerely love this country in spite of all its perversity and its materialism. There is a sincerity here which pleases me, and once well directed, it gives you souls both noble and generous; one cannot regret the time and the toil they cost us."[10]

The one event that marred Bishop Miege's retirement plans was the death of his beloved older brother Urban in mid-December 1874. The following January he wrote to Canon Alliaudi:

It has pleased the divine Master to call to himself this much-loved brother, whose advice and prayers have been such great help to me and to the family. May His holy will be done! I will try by my prayers to pay the debt of gratitude that I owe to his kindness and to the sincerity of his truly fraternal love. Tears and sorrow are quite natural, when I lose what I held most dear in the world, but I well know that this is not what he is asking of me. One must pray for him that the good Father grants him the happiness and the joys of Paradise.

I am firmly convinced that he is already praying for us; but in case the divine Judge has found some imperfections to atone for, let us help him with our prayers and good works to hasten his happiness.[11]

At the time of Urban's death, the bishop had the following advice to give to his nephew and to his family:

The loneliness you and the family complain about is quite natural. Your good uncle has seen you grow up . . . He has been an instrument of Divine Providence for the good of the family. Such a loss does not repair itself; but it is softened by going back to the source of all good, who gives consolations and sends afflictions to encourage us and to try us, and to make us understand that we are still in the breach struggling and fighting for victory; it will come; patience and courage!

I firmly trust that the division of the property will take place amicably, as is fitting between brothers, and that all will imitate the charity and the goodwill of him who did everything and sacrificed all for them. There is no thought that consoles me more than that which brings to mind all my brothers and sisters living in perfect harmony, mutually encouraging one another by their good advice, their good example, and their union. It is easily the truest happiness one can enjoy on earth. I hope it will be the lot of all my nephews and nieces.[12]

In his letter of January 1875, Father Miege also tells Canon Alliaudi how sincerely devoted he himself was to the priests, the men and women religious, and the Catholics of Kansas. "For their part they have always shown me more consideration than I deserved and more goodwill than I had the right to expect. It is not then they who have brought about my resignation. It is justice and truth that cause me to speak in this manner."[13] An example of the esteem in which Bishop Miege was held by his people may be gathered from the following testimonial:

Right Reverend Bishop Miege

At a meeting of the Catholics of Leavenworth City, Kansas, held on the 10th day of January, 1875, the following resolutions regarding the departure of Right Reverend

Bishop Miege from amongst us were unanimously adopted:—Whereas in the exercise of a just and legitimate power, our much loved Bishop Miege has been called from a diocese which has so richly reaped the benefit of his untiring zeal, his fervent piety, and his keen penetrating sagacity exercised during more than twenty years of arduous duty which have brought out of a chaotic wilderness a living tangible spiritual power: Be it therefore—Resolved: That we, his humble parishioners, meet this change with heavy hearts and saddened spirits, that our warmest love and sympathies and affections follow him into his new sphere of duty. Resolved: That in his departure the Catholics of Kansas lose a faithful shepherd, whose eye was ever open to the spiritual interests and advancement of his flock; a wise counselor, whose clear, sound sagacious advice was never withheld from those who sought it; and a sincere and devoted friend whose unswerving fidelity to the claims of friendship was the wonder and admiration of all who were brought within its circle. Resolved: That while as loyal Catholics we submit, as is our duty, to the necessity which has made this step necessary or desirable, we still deplore the circumstances which have induced our beloved Bishop to resign the high dignity of the Episcopacy and retire to the humbler walks and duties of his order. That, inasmuch as the step has been taken, and we have not been consulted therein, while deploring his determination, our warmest affections shall go with him wheresoever duty shall call him, our profoundest respect and deepest gratitude shall follow him while life shall last, and our love and respect for him as Catholics is shared by the people of Kansas generally, who in the past twenty years have learned to know him for his sterling worth and energy in the upbuilding of the material interests of the State, his devotion to its people and to their interests and honor during the many struggles that have marked the history of our young Commonwealth. Resolved: That we cheerfully acquiesce in the selection of the Right Reverend Bishop Fink as the successor of Bishop Miege, and in giving him our cordial support and just obedience we will but recognize the judgement of our former Bishop in his selection. Resolved: That a copy of these resolutions, correctly engrossed, be forwarded to the Right Reverend Bishop Miege at Saint Louis, Missouri, by the Committee.

Owen Duffy	James A. McGonigle
Thos. P. Fenlon	Edmund Walsh
Jno. Hannon	M. S. Thomas
Edward Carroll	Edward Morgan
Thos. Jones	John McCormick
Michael Greelish	Patrick Gilston
P. Geraughty, Secretary	W. Thomas, Chairman[14]

A similar address was drawn up by the Catholic clergy of Kansas assembled at Topeka, Kansas, on January 4, 1875. It reads in part:

> The clergy of Kansas feel it a bounden duty to give a formal expression to our regret at the sad event which has at once deprived the American Church of a great prelate, the priests of Kansas of a kind father, and the laity committed to his care of a true and faithful guide. And, moreover, sensible of the many claims which our late bishop has on our gratitude; proud as we will ever be of the memory of one who has been the pioneer of Catholicity in these Western States, one who has left after him so many monuments of zeal and piety; grateful for the hospitality and paternal affection with which he forever behaved towards his clergy. We take this occasion of paying him this tribute of our heartfelt love and respect.[15]

On Tuesday, December 15, 1874, the *Daily Times* announced that the citizens of Leavenworth, without regard to creed, would regret to hear of the departure of Right Reverend J. B. Miege. "He came here when a few huts comprised what was known as Leavenworth, and the cathedral, the hospital and the academy attest his faith in the future of our city. He was universally beloved, and the Catholics of Kansas will sustain a severe loss in his departure."[16]

When the *Leavenworth Commercial* asserted that Miege "retired from Kansas and the Episcopacy on account of the pressing debt due upon the Cathedral," Irish-born Father

Thomas Ambrose Butler wrote a letter to the editor of the rival paper, the *Daily Times,* calling the assertion a "gross libel" and insisting there was not a word of truth in the statement. One who had faced every known danger for twenty-four years from the Missouri to the Rocky Mountains, he continued, could not possibly "act as a coward." Rather, the incentive to retire "arose from a deep feeling of true Christian humility and a desire to return to the ranks of the Religious Order which claimed him as her love." Butler recalls how Miege tried to resign even before his consecration. He tells how, in 1866, the bishops who met at the Council of Baltimore refused even to examine his reasons for resignation. He further mentions that the clergy of Kansas appointed a committee in 1870, when Bishop Miege went to the Vatican Council, begging the pope to refuse his resignation. Butler concluded: "The man who labored in the vineyard of the Catholic Church of Kansas for one quarter of a century has gone back to the holy family that adopted him in his youth. May the blessings of Heaven fall upon his soul!"[17]

Thirty years later the Reverend Anton Kuhls told how Bishop Miege left his beloved cathedral and city "without bidding adieu to anyone, going with one brother to the depot at 4 A.M. so that no one might see him or make any demonstration." Father Kuhls mentions that he left his possessions, even his pectoral cross and his gold watch, in Leavenworth. Words could not describe the profound sadness experienced by the bishop's departure, especially by the clergy. He then gave the following beautiful eulogy:

> No bishop of America was ever revered and loved like Bishop J.B. Miege—alike by priests and people—by Catholics and Protestants. He was a father to his priests. His house was the priests' home and his hospitality was endless. He had a word of encouragement for everyone . . . . As long as memory will last, his name will be held in benediction. . . . During all his administration there never was an unkind word between him and his priests. He never dipped his pen in acid when he wrote to his clergy.[18]

Apparently Father Miege failed to make his departure from Leavenworth entirely alone. Somehow his beloved priestly co-worker Father Butler got word of the time and saw him off at the station.[19]

In a letter to Canon Alliaudi written in early January, Father Miege tells us that he was then at St. Louis University. From the tone of the letter we gather that he was not at all well. He wrote: "I feel that I am growing old; my legs seem to get benumbed and make faces when they have to walk. Thus it is time to make provisions for the quiet voyage whose end cannot be very far away. Help me with your good prayers, my dear friend, so that all of us may get together where there will be no separation, where there will be only happiness and joy for the saints and the elect of God."[20]

A month later Father Miege still did not know definitely what he would have to do nor the part of the United States where he would be working. He was waiting for a letter from the Father General to inform him on these matters. Earlier, the general had asked him to choose among Missouri, Louisiana, and Maryland. He replied that he was willing to go wherever he was sent. At the same time he felt there was a good chance that he would be staying in the Missouri province, his home in the New World. However, Louisiana was another possibility, since it was under the Lyons province to which he had belonged before coming to America.[21]

After six months of well merited rest at St. Louis University, Father Miege was sent by his superiors to Woodstock College in Maryland. There he was charged with giving spiritual direction to the students and missionary aspirants. Apparently, the work, together with the rest, was proving beneficial since he informed his nephew Joseph-Eugene, in late December, that his health was not bad though, like a thermometer, it had its ups and downs. He was still having trouble with his legs. However, as he put it: "I make them march every day so that they do not lose their good habits."[22]

This same letter indicates what happened to the missing South American letters. Father Miege asked his nephew to send him any such letters that were still in Urban's files, beginning with the correspondence from Chile. He requested that everything else he had written be burned. The Chilean letters were indeed sent; fortunately, for us, the others were not committed to the flames.[23]

From a letter written to Canon Alliaudi we learn a bit more on how Father Miege passed the time at Woodstock. He referred to the year since his retirement as being one of "real peace and happiness," spent in directing and encouraging young Jesuits by preparing them for the apostolate. He devoted the rest of the time reacquainting himself with the rules and constitutions of the Society of Jesus. He considered the work to be most practical and thanked God for having given him the occasion to dedicate himself to it. He mentioned, too, that his health had been generally very good. Headaches bothered him at times, but never for more than a day or two.[24]

Father Miege also informed his friend on the coming centennial of the Declaration of Independence. It would be celebrated at Philadelphia with more pomp and ceremony than the opening and closing of the recent exposition there. Recently, he had received a facsimile of the document that was originally signed and read at Philadelphia. He promised to send the copy to Canon Alliaudi so that he could read it for himself.[25]

It was in the midst of all this, while Father Miege was getting acclimated to his new position, that his superiors asked him to go to Detroit to serve as rector-president of the new Jesuit college, which was about to be founded by the Right Reverend Caspar H. Borgess, bishop of Detroit.

— 15 —

THE DETROIT COLLEGE PRESIDENT

There is much ado nowadays about second vocations in life. Early retirees are advised not to let themselves stagnate. Suggestions on how to keep oneself occupied is dispensed regularly. Actually, the Jesuits never had much trouble staying busy. Most of them have preferred to serve the Lord as long as possible. Father John Baptist Miege was no exception. When he was asked by his superiors to work with Bishop Borgess of Detroit in founding a new college, he responded like the old trooper that he was.

Perhaps the first time Detroiters would have heard of John Baptist Miege was from an advertisement that appeared in the *Western Home Journal* on August 25, 1877, and for several weeks thereafter. It read:

> The Detroit College. This education Institution under the direction of the Fathers of the Society of Jesus will be opened on the first Monday of September. The charge for Tuition in the Academic Department per session of Ten Months will be $40.00. Payment to be made quarterly in advance. For further information apply to Rev. J. B. Miege, S.J., 353 Jefferson Avenue, Detroit, Michigan.

The man chiefly responsible for the foundation of the new college was Bishop Caspar Henry Borgess, who came to

Detroit in 1870 as successor to Bishop Peter Paul Lefevre. Shortly thereafter the new bishop, in a pastoral letter, made manifest his interest in the work of Catholic education. Seeing the need for an institution of higher learning, he asked the Basilians "to keep open and maintain a High School and College for Day-Scholars in the City of Detroit, in which a thorough course of Commercial &, at least, a preparatory course of Classical education shall be given."[1] When, at the time, the Basilians were unable to staff such a college, the bishop turned to the Jesuits. This was not surprising since, as a student at Saint Xavier College in Cincinnati, Borgess had come to love and respect the Jesuits, a feeling that deepened during his work in the chancery in Cincinnati. The bishop first discussed the possibility of an establishment with the exiled German Jesuits of the Buffalo mission. When they were unable to accept his offer, he turned to the Jesuits of the St. Louis-based Missouri province. They readily granted their approval.

Father General Peter Beckx, S.J., also gave his permission for the projected college. He wrote to Father Thomas O'Neil, the Missouri provincial: "Your Reverence thinks together with his consultors that the wishes of the Right Reverend Bishop of Detroit ought to be complied with and a start made with a college. I agree with your reverence, since I am convinced that competent instructors are available. . . ."[2] A month later Father Beckx told Father O'Neil that he had made an excellent choice in Bishop Miege but cautioned him not to let this appointment work to the detriment of Woodstock College, which played such an important part in the formation of young Jesuits. Apparently, the Father General still considered the aging Miege an appropriate role model to the young Jesuits at Woodstock.[3]

It is surprising that the final agreement between the bishop and the provincial should have been reached so quickly. After several letters were exchanged, Father O'Neil presented the document to his consultors for approval and formal signature in early April 1877. In return for establishing a college, the Society of Jesus would be given, in fee simple, the cathedral church of SS. Peter and Paul with its surrounding property:

> On condition that the said party of the second part and his successors in the office of Provincial, shall establish

and maintain in the said City of Detroit a College or School for the education of youth. But if at any time the said party of the second part or anyone of his successors in the office should deem it necessary or advisable to change the location of said College or School, and establish it on some other part of the City of Detroit, the said party of the first part hereby grants permission and gives authority to build a church near the new College or School when such change shall be decided upon or effected, and to organize there a parish in such manner and with such limits as shall be agreed upon by the parties to this contract or their successors in the office at the time. And moreover if by reason of such change in the location of the said College or School, or for other valid reasons, the said party of the second part or any one of his successors in the office of Provincial, should judge it necessary or advisable to sell or dispose of the property in this manner conveyed to him, he shall be at liberty to do so, provided both parties shall agree that the church edifice of SS. Peter & Paul is no longer needed for the Catholics within the present limits of said congregation; but the said party of the second part binds himself and his successors in office at the time, to expend the proceeds of such sale within the Diocese of Detroit.[4]

The above document was signed April 5, 1877. On June 1, a small advance group of Jesuits, including Father Miege, arrived in Detroit, excited and eager to begin work on their new undertaking. The college diary gives their names: in addition to Miege, Fathers Eugene Brady, S.J., James Walshe, S.J., and Edward Higgins, S.J. The diary also notes that they were "ready for instant work." How ready we gather from a brief entry on June 2, a Saturday, which declares that all were "employed in the confessional."[5]

On Friday, June 8, *The Evening News* ran an interesting article entitled "The Society of Jesus," telling its readers who the Jesuits were and what they planned to do in Detroit. The article began: "The average American who has received his principal notions of the Jesuit from the thrilling pages of Eugene Sue, or the fiery pronunciamentos of Mazzini, must have experienced a small thrill of horror when he read the recent announcement in the *News* that this dreaded order had actually established a branch in Detroit." The article then went on to say that "those who look on the Jesuit as the embodiment of pride, arrogance, ambition, craft and cruelty, would no doubt be astonished to meet the four quiet, unostentatious, courteous, learned and gentlemanly persons who, with so little display or advertisement installed themselves at the cathedral last week." There followed a brief account of the order, its rule of life, its vows, and its work throughout the world. The article concluded with a short biographical sketch of the four newly arrived Jesuits. Referring to Father Miege, *The Evening News* aptly remarked: "He wore the mitre very successfully for 22 years, and built up the Catholic Church in Kansas in a most gratifying manner."[6]

The summer months did not slip by easily for the little band of Jesuits now firmly settled in the "cathedral" rectory. In addition to the regular church services, in which they all did their share, there was the matter of preparing a plan of studies for the college and interviewing prospective students and their parents. The most crucial problem that presented itself to President Miege and his faculty was finding a suitable location and classroom building. As late as June 16 the college diary stated that "no desirable property being at the nonce for sale, it is concluded that our residence must furnish room for college purposes."[7] Unfortunately, the St. Louis authorities did not heed Father General Beckx's advice given in the very letter in which he approved opening the college. There he cautioned the Fathers against burdening themselves unduly. Hence, they should *first* buy the property near the church even before they take up residence. Holding classes in their place of residence would not have been a happy solution to the problem. Fortunately, Father Miege and his colleagues were spared that eventuality. On July 16, an entry in the diary tells us that the old Trowbridge House, at 362 Jefferson Avenue, located on the south side of the street opposite the Jesuit residence, had been secured through the services of W.B. Thomas at the "very reasonable cost of $21,500."[8] According to the *The Evening News,* the lot had a frontage of 110 feet and a depth of 200 feet. Work on the house, the *News* added, would begin immediately in order to be ready when classes opened the first Monday of September.[9]

It was decided that the spacious drawing rooms on the first floor of the mansion would make very suitable classrooms.

Trowbridge House, the first classroom building of
Detroit College. Courtesy University of Detroit
Archives.

On the second floor partitions were taken down, and the area
renovated to provide additional smaller classrooms and some
office space. Fifty double desks were ordered at $3.75 each.
They arrived on August 29, three days before classes began.
Apparently the work of restoration, supervised by Father
Hugo J. Erley, was done with the help of three of his fellow
Jesuits and three professional carpenters. For a week or so
before classes began, seven weary men laid their tools aside
each evening at ten o'clock under a new gold-lettered sign
that proclaimed the building to be the Detroit College.

By the time classes were to begin, President Miege's faculty
had increased to nine. Father Erley was Prefect of Studies or
Dean. Fathers Brady and Walshe were assistant pastors in the
church, where they also cared for the spiritual welfare of the
students. Two Jesuit scholastics, Joseph Grimmelsman and
Augustine Effinger, taught second academic and third academic,
respectively. Both performed their routine teaching duties
before ordination. Father Joseph F. Real was placed in charge
of the class of rudiments, which covered beginning Latin, basic
math, and English. Brothers William Forbes and Henry Veith
were buyer and receptionist, respectively, for the college.

In mid-July the *Detroit Free Press* discussed the type of education to be given by the Jesuits. Since, by then, an authentic

prospectus had been printed and distributed under Father Miege's name, we use it here as our source. From it we learn that the plan of studies would include "the doctrines and evidences of the Catholic Religion, Logic, Metaphysics, Ethics, Astronomy, Natural Philosophy, Chemistry, Bookkeeping, Arithmetic, the Latin, Greek, English, French, and German Languages."[10] According to the *Prospectus,* frequent examinations were to be given, and it would be one of President Miege's duties to inform parents how their sons were faring at any given time.[11]

On September 3, 1877, sixty students reported and were classified. The next day they met at the Jesuit residence and were taken across Jefferson Avenue to be shown to their classrooms. The college diary described them as "a fine set of youths." Among them were the sons of many prominent Detroit families—Groesbeck, Van Antwerp, Campau, Roney, St. Aubin, Russell, McDougall, Dinan, and other well-known names. The college catalog for 1877–78 had a final list of eighty-four students in attendance that year. The figure remained the same for the next two years, but by 1885 it had risen to 243 students.

Perhaps the greatest wonder of the undertaking is how Father Miege and his colleagues could run a college of eighty-four students those initial three years at $40 per student, for a total of $3,360 per year. The debt for the Trowbridge House and its improvements came to thirty thousand dollars. At 6 percent this would have left an interest alone of $1,800, which meant that only $1,560 remained for ordinary running expenses. Strictly speaking, the Jesuits received no salary for their work at the college, which was run on a family basis. If any money remained after expenses, it was used for the support of the Fathers. Whatever else was needed would have had to come from free-will offerings and from pastoral services rendered on weekends throughout the city.

In a letter to Canon Alliaudi, written in 1878 at the end of the first school year, Father Miege mentions a previous letter in which he had given his friend a detailed account of the situation in Detroit. Unfortunately, that letter seems to have disappeared. However, subsequent letters of 1878 and 1879 give us his impressions of Detroit and his work there. First, Father Miege did not like Detroit's weather. He told his friend that, while Detroit is a northern city, as is proven in the winter months, it has "certain days in summer when one would think himself under the Equator." This was the case at the time of his writing. It was so hot, he wrote, that one had to put on gloves so as not to wet the paper. Still, compared with Detroit, St. Louis fared worse. In just one day there, forty persons died from heat exhaustion. In Detroit the highest number of people overcome by the heat on any given day was eight. In this same letter Father Miege mentions that justice to the number of students demanded that he add a floor to the college. He no doubt was referring to renovating the already existing third floor of the Trowbridge residence. Characteristically, he added the hope that "the good God continue to bless our enterprise that is destined to do a lot of good and to repair the gaps that the lack of Catholic education has caused in our town." He also referred to the services rendered in the church during the first year alone. Miege, along with four priests, had listened to some forty thousand confessions and gave more than thirty-six thousand communions, in addition to sermons, retreats, triduums, and novenas.[12]

In another letter, probably written a year later, Father Miege told Canon Alliandi that affairs in Detroit were going along quite nicely. The college was solidly founded and the church continued to be well attended. He added an interesting bit of trivia. It seems that an "Irishman" in the parish was "scandalized" by the fact that the only carillon in town was in the steeple of a Protestant church. Accordingly, he went out and bought a nine-bell carillon for SS. Peter and Paul's Church, which cost him some 16,500 francs. The bells, Miege added, were to be blessed by Bishop Borgess the Tuesday or Wednesday after Easter. It was to be a very solemn affair. He continues:

> We will have a hundred voices, which will be accompanied by the organ and the carillon in the chanting of the *Te Deum*. We will also have, before the *Te Deum*, a formal discourse by one of our Fathers who is considered to be one of the finest orators in the United States. And anybody who wants to see and hear all this will have to pay 2 francs 50 to get into the Church. We are hoping to realize from 4,000 to 5,000 francs by this festivity.

Lest the good canon be scandalized by the entrance fee, Father Miege hastened to inform him that this was commonly done in the United States and that he would see it in France "if you separate the State from the Church there."[13]

This is not the place to examine in detail the impact of the Jesuits on post-Tridentine liturgy. We might point out, however, that, beginning with the Gesù in Rome, most Jesuit churches were built in the Baroque style, with altar and pulpit prominently in the midst of the people, a lengthened communion rail, confessionals easily accessible, and a well-lit interior so that the faithful could take part in the services. Little wonder that the Baroque is sometimes identified with the Jesuits. The "Baroque Oratorio" is also at times referred to as the Jesuit style in music. Throughout Europe the Jesuits were famous for their magnificent liturgies, particularly their elaborate funerals of prominent men and women. We seem to catch an echo of this in SS. Peter and Paul's Church when, in February 1878, the college gathered to celebrate a solemn requiem mass for Father Miege's good friend, the recently deceased Pope Pius IX.

The local press reported that the "Acolythical Society," a group of young college students who served the priests at Mass and on other occasions, was present at the time "in full force wearing black scarfs"—no doubt worn over their usual purple cassocks trimmed in red with white lace surplices. The report continued:

> The church was all draped in mourning. The light was excluded so that the somber appearance lent much to the solemnity of the celebration. The size of the church added to the effect of the decorations; the whole appearance was simply grand and imposing. In front of the sanctuary stood the magnificent catafalque. It was three stories high and covered with the richest velvet braided with silver. The whole was strewn with the choicest flowers in great profusion. The area surrounding the catafalque was a forest of tropical plants. Nearly 1,000 lights and jets of gas mingling with those presented a most striking picture, and so impressed the people that they could with difficulty withdraw their gaze from it . . . . Mozart's grand Requiem Mass was sung. . . .[14]

Father Miege's health had not been good during his three years in Detroit. The climate and, no doubt, financial worries, together with work in the college and the church, all contributed to his illness. Being religious superior of his colleagues did not help. Still, in spite of ill health, he remained his charming self and won the goodwill of everybody concerned. His retirement, though regretted, was not surprising. At the end of the 1879–80 school year, his superiors decided to send him to Saint Xavier's College in Cincinnati. There he would teach moral theology, give "exhortations" to the community, and hear confessions. Fortunately, for his sake, before assuming his new assignment, a counter order arrived making his beloved Woodstock College his final earthly home.[15]

16

THE LAST YEARS

Father Miege had a great liking for Woodstock College, with its trees, its gardens, and its well-kept grounds. He had a particular affection for the Lourdes grotto, which he was wont to visit daily. His work at Woodstock was much the same as when he left in 1877 to become the founding president of Detroit College. He gave exhortations and heard confessions and accounts of conscience of the philosophers and theologians, who then numbered 125. While his duties required a lot of time and energy, he felt he could manage it "with the help of our Master and his very holy Mother." Meanwhile his health continued to be reasonably good.[1]

During his stay at Woodstock, Father Miege continued his interest in American politics. A good example of his knowledge of current affairs is contained in a letter to Canon Alliaudi in December 1880:

The United States are very tranquil for the moment. The elections did not make as much noise as ordinarily, and the Democrats are accepting their defeat with astonishing resignation to the will of the people. The Republicans, then, will have the management of affairs and the key to the treasury for four more years. And as the rascals are very clever knaves and adroit jugglers, you can reckon that they will show that dollars are round since they should roll, but not roll for the common good, but into the pocket of this riff-raff. The honest Democrats console themselves in thinking that, if their party had won the Presidency, the difference in the matter of justice and honesty would have been striking. There is where we stand. For the rest the prosperity of the country is really extraordinary, and the statistics of our newspapers are correct. You fat bourgeois Europeans will be obliged to buy our wheat, our corn, our meat and our animals, without counting our machinery of all kinds, our sugar and our cotton. That goes to show that material prosperity is making great progress, but unhappily spiritual prosperity, it is much to be feared, recedes and will recede in the same proportion as the other advances. Poor America! I love it much and it is this that causes me to fear for her. But God is good, and I trust he will not strike except to heal. A bad sign for me is that they are beginning to speak very freely of a dictator and even of an emperor. It is enough to have an entirely moldy administration without having grand titles to cover tyranny. . . .[2]

If there is anything special to be noted throughout Miege's letters, it is his solid faith and great trust in God and the Blessed Mother. When he heard that his niece Sister Saint-Louis was suffering severely, he expressed his grief to Alliaudi and then added:

Tell her to have good courage, and not to lose any of all the merit of a perfect resignation. All this will make a lovely crown in heaven. I am praying for her and for all the family at least three times a day, and I frequently ask our holy and good Mother to bless and protect them.[3]

Father Miege also told his friend that, while his health was not bad, his legs were somewhat remiss in that they did not do their duty as briskly as one might wish. What was needed was patience and resignation, and since he preached this to his goddaughter it was only fitting that he practice it himself. He went on to say that it was fortunate his work did not demand much movement. When the weather was good he walked for about an hour in the late afternoon. The rest of the time he spent reading, writing, and chatting about spiritual things with his young folks. How quickly the time passed, he would comment in amazement.[4]

On March 4, 1881, Father Miege drew up and signed his last will and testament probably to avoid the possibility of any litigation after his death:

> In the name of the Father and of the Son and of the Holy Ghost. Amen.
>
> I the undersigned John B. Miege of Woodstock College county of Baltimore State of Maryland being of sound mind and memory do now make publick and declare this as my last will and testament, hereby evoking and annulling all and any wills & testaments heretofore made and published.
>
> First, I order that all my just debts be paid.
>
> Second, all my real estate lying and situate in the State of Kansas of which I may be possessed at the time of my death and all rights and interests to and in said property, I leave bequeath and make over to Louis M. Fink of the City of Leavenworth, known as the Roman Catholic Bishop of Leavenworth in the State of Kansas.
>
> Third, I nominate and appoint John F. Cunningham of Topeka, Kansas, to be the executor of this my last will & testament and direct the court not to require any bonds from him for the faithful performance of his duties.
>
> In witness whereof I have hereunto set my hand and affixed my seal this fourth day of March An Dni. 1881.[5]

After 1880 the correspondence of the aging Jesuit became rarer and shorter. Garin mentions that he could not find a single letter written to his friends during 1881. Then, in January 1882, Miege wrote to Canon Alliaudi to wish him a happy New Year and to commiserate with him on the required retirement of their mutual friend the Curé. He told Alliaudi that things were moving along nicely. The winter was mild, and peace prevailed in the various states. Hope for material prosperity was everywhere. He added that it was not yet decided what to do with President Garfield's assassin, Charles J. Guiteau—Garfield had died on September 19, 1881, two months after being shot at a Washington, D.C., train station—

but that folks hoped he would be hanged, which, in fact, he was later that year. In this same letter he enclosed a census report from 1880 that reported the population of the different states, the number of Catholics and other denominations, the produce of the land, and similar information. He ended by saying that he could not complain too much about his health but that he did not have much to brag about either. Though his strength was lessening he had no pain.[6]

In November of that same year he again wrote to Alliaudi. "I am going to command my sloth," he began, "to take the pen resolutely and write to you as lengthily as possible." He was beginning to understand, he wrote, the difficulty his brother Urban had, during the last years of his life, writing to him so faithfully in spite of his infirmities. He again referred to the peace and tranquility that prevailed in the United States, and indeed, one could say, in the whole world at the time. Excellent harvests and a very brisk commerce were in large part the cause of this joy. Such good fortune was expected to last into the following year. Then, characteristically, he added: "The good God should have many accounts to settle with us Americans; and if he does it rigorously he will send us a great scourge, which I am constantly afraid will break out. Let us hope that our Lord in his infinite charity will not strike except to heal and to convert."[7]

Father Miege believed that the success of Catholicism in America was due, in part, to immigration, although how much longer it would last was anyone's guess. Although the better lands had long since been taken, there remained millions of less fertile lands, which could be bought at comparatively low prices. Once all available land was claimed, he estimated there would be a hundred million inhabitants in the United States, thirty million of whom would be Catholic.[8]

Writing in the early 1880s, a time when big business was just getting under way in the United States, Miege could not foresee the rise of the cities with their industries that would offer employment to millions of immigrants in the years to come.[9]

He added a somewhat curious comment in his letter to Alliaudi. He hoped that the number of Catholics would remain sufficiently large to make them respected but never so large that they could think of tampering with the constitution of a government that had made so many of them rich and happy. The Germans, he thought, would be the first to complain about the freedom that the U. S. constitution grants. They did so in 1853 and it was that which led to the persecution of Catholics and foreigners at the time. He compared the situation to that in France where sectarians governed the republic. Apparently Miege's love for his adopted country prompted him to fear the emergence of a Catholic equivalent of a Know Nothing party that would rival the earlier Protestant Anglo-Saxon (German?) group. However, he felt that at the time of his writing the promoters of high politics were showing themselves very reserved to the satisfaction of all folks of good heart.[10]

Father Miege admitted to the canon that he was growing old and more feeble by the day. But he insisted that it was not due to added weight. "A word to those," he wrote, "who accused me last year of not being able to walk because my legs had too much to carry. I do not weigh more than in 1870, but the machinery is growing weaker."[11]

Old and feeble though he was, Father Miege continued to be interested in his work and in the well-being of his friends. When he heard that Canon Alliaudi had been named editor of the revived paper, *l'Echo des Alpes,* he hastened to congratulate him and to wish him well in the undertaking. Also, upon learning that an estate had been bought back home to be used for a Catholic school, he congratulated the canon as well as the Curé Marjolet and the parishioners of Chevron. He was so pleased when he heard of the proposed school that he asked the Father Rector of Woodstock College, John Bapst, for an alms to send to his old friends. He was almost embarrassed to tell them that the rector gave him "the little sum of 150 francs," which he enclosed. He added: "If I could I would gladly pay a debt of gratitude that our good curé has caused me to contract; but unfortunately it will be necessary to wait." He explained that the reason for the smallness of the gift was that the Maryland province had contracted a debt of more than twelve hundred thousand francs to construct Woodstock College, which still had to be paid.[12]

Father Miege's next letter was written the following March to Marjolet, Curé of Chevron. He began by telling Marjolet that the poor state of his health was forcing him to use the services of a secretary. On Septuagesima Sunday he had suffered a stroke, which paralyzed his left side. Since then he was unable to leave his room except rarely and only with the help of two persons. What grieved him most was that he was deprived of the happiness of celebrating the Holy Sacrifice of the Mass. He asked Marjolet for prayers and then added:

> Before acting like a beggar, it is more just that I offer you my most sincere thanks for your kindness towards me. Believe me, my very dear Curé, none of the many benefits for which I am your debtor have escaped my memory; I am making an effort as best as I can to pay the debts of gratitude that I owe you. . . .[13]

Finally, on October 17, 1883, the venerable father wrote his last letter to Canon Alliaudi. He thanked him for having feted their mutual friend the Curé of Chevron on the occasion of the fiftieth anniversary of his ordination to the priesthood. He again expressed the hope that they would not retire the good curé, since that would be bound to kill him. Finally, he asked that his respect and his affection be extended to all his friends. He then added: "The strength of my left side and my arms is diminishing. May the holy will of God be done. When he tells me to go I shall depart with confidence in his infinite goodness and mercy!"[14]

In December 1883, John Bapst wrote to Sister Saint-Louis to make known the condition of her uncle. He told her of Father Miege's stroke and his partial paralysis. He mentioned that, without being completely cured, he was well enough to say Mass and spend some time in the garden each day. He concluded by saying that his mind was still clear and that, in spite of the paralysis, he was as joyful as ever. He continued to edify the community by his patience and his good example.[15]

Finally, on August 3, 1884, the same Father Rector informed Sister Saint-Louis of the death of her dear uncle:

> Dear Sister in Jesus Christ:
> Good Father Miege has left us for heaven, we have all the right to hope for it, on July 21, at 4:30 in the morning. The paralysis had affected his intestines for more than a week and brought about a fatal dysentery. The good father received the last sacraments, and kept his consciousness right up to the end. After having administered the last sacraments, the Father Provincial asked him

if he did not have some good advice to give to all the young Fathers who surrounded him. The good prelate answered simply: "Tell them to be charitable!" He never ceased to edify us by his well-known piety. He ardently wished for several months to be dissolved to go with Christ . . . He is interred here in the cemetery with his brothers in religion; his funeral took place in our chapel, following the custom of our Society. . . . [16]

When he heard of Father Miege's death, James Defouri, vicar general of the Diocese of Santa Fe, wrote:

A great light of the Church has just been extinguished. A man of God, a model priest and religious, a Saintly Bishop has passed away in the quiet of Woodstock College, Howard Co., Maryland. A man preeminent in virtue and science yet with the simplicity of a child, an unconquerable spirit of retirement; the violet with all its fragrance. I speak of the much loved Rt. Rev. J. B. Miege. I knew him well. I was living under his ever hospitable roof. [17]

The kindly old Kansas missionary, Father Paul Ponziglione, S.J., added:

. . . the world will never forget him. Kansas will remember him for years to come. The Cathedral, the Academy, the Hospital, and the schools he put up are standing monuments that speak for him more brilliantly than any tongue can do. But of all the monuments he leaves, the Christianity, which he established in Kansas should be that which more eloquently than any other shall speak of him to future generations. [18]

Father Miege's colleagues at Woodstock College showed their esteem for their brother in a lengthy obituary published in *Woodstock Letters*. The final paragraph reads:

It is indeed difficult to do even scant justice to the leading features of this truly patriarchal character. Fr. Miege was a holy priest, a humble religious and a zealous Bishop. His presence ever proved an unfailing spell,

charming the young into a confiding freedom of inter-
course, and his older friends into a mingled veneration
and love for his great social and religious virtues. He had
a smile and a hearty reception for everybody, simply
because all had a deep share in his sympathy, and none
ever proved the object of his suspicion or dislike. With
the sad and dejected he was always discriminate. He per-
ceived, one would say, intuitively, where there was a
dangerous or harmful melancholy, and none knew better
than he what to say and how to say it. To these afflicted
friends, he was really a father; but, when trifles disturbed
the mind, his raillery was simply baffling. It gave no
quarter, admitted no explanation, but provoked an entire
oblivion, or a ludicrous recollection of the little things
that sometimes make a man miserable. He so adjusted
his attention to everybody, that it was a perfect pastime
to entertain him, and a treat to enjoy the favor of his
company; disliking unnecessary distinctions, his great
soul sympathized equally with all who found in him a
kind father and an unswerving friend.[19]

One could go on. A fitting conclusion to our story might be
a homily preached by the Very Reverend William T. J. Boland,
pastor of the "Old Cathedral" in Leavenworth. The occasion
was the celebration of the centennial of the Diocese of Kansas
City, Kansas, April 24, 1950. After a lengthy summary of
Miege's life and work, Father Boland concluded:

Possessing as he did the happy combination of Alpine
virility proper to the Savoyards, tempered by a French
finesse of manner, he was peculiarly fitted to be the first
resident ecclesiastical superior of a virgin country called
the "Great Plains."
   In his career as Vicar Apostolic there can be found all
that was pioneer—self-sacrifice, suffering, energy, initiative,
ruggedness, fortitude, versatility. In laying the foundation
for Catholicity in Kansas, Nebraska, and Colorado, he did
the work of the pioneer, clearing the way, breaking the
soil, and forming solid, unpretentious groundwork on
which his successors could and did build. He did more
than adapt himself to pioneer ways: He uplifted them.
He brought a refining influence into the careless, unorga-

nized life of the territory by the establishment of academies conducted by religious. His presence in Kansas supplied a moral and intellectual force during an epoch of fraud, lawlessness, and terror.

Finally, he had a genius for friendship which included the young and the old, the cultured and the illiterate, those of his own fold and those outside of it. His interests were as wide as the territory he governed. His chief contribution to the West can never be fully evaluated nor measured, because it was the intangible force—personal influence. Love always expresses itself in service. He who lives forever in the minds and hearts of his countrymen has loved humanity through humble, daily service in kindly deeds to the unfortunate of earth. . . . History is not an impartial critic. By reason of material prosperity one may be considered great in his day and generation, but greatness is often interred with his bones. We, celebrating this centennial today, feel that the name of Bishop John Baptist Miege has left its mark on Kansas, because he loved his fellow men and saw in them the image of God.[20]

And so ends our story of the shepherd boy born in the shadow of the Swiss Alps, who was to become a Jesuit and, after his ordination to the priesthood in 1847, a missionary in the United States. Ordained a bishop in St. Louis at the early age of thirty-six, he was charged with caring for the spiritual needs of the vicariate of the Indian Territory, an area comprising some 500,000 square miles and containing about one thousand Catholics. Of that vast territory today, Kansas alone contains two and a half million people, with a Catholic population of 371,091. And Bishop Miege was there at the beginning of it all. As we ponder over his life, we cannot help but love this man with a heart as big as his 250 pounds. His was not an easy life. He suffered from the severe cold of winter and the intense heat of summer as he traveled from one end of his diocese to the other on horseback or in his prairie schooner. But it is on the shoulders of people such as Bishop Miege that rests the greatness of our country today.

NOTES

Chapter 1: Early Years

1. For the most part, Miege used the French spelling of his name—
   Jean Baptiste *Miége* with the acute accent. Some of his friends
   and biographers use the grave accent. American papers and documents, however, use the English spelling. For the sake of
   avoiding confusion we shall do the same throughout.

2. See the Woodstock College Press publication, *The Woodstock
   Letters: A Record of Current Events and Historical Notes
   Connected with the Colleges and Missions of the Society of Jesus* 13
   (1884): 396–99.

3. Joseph Garin, *Les Évêques et Prêtres de Chevron* (Albertville,
   France: Libraire M. Papet, 1936), 46. By the same author, see
   *Notices Biographiques sur Mgr. J.-B. Miége Premier Vicaire
   Apostolique du Kansas* (Moûtiers, France: Imprimerie Cane
   Soeurs, 1886), 2, 14. Savoy and Nice were ceded to France by
   the Treaty of Turin, 24 March 1860. The Upper or Northern por-
   tion of Savoy (Haute Savoie) had been French-speaking for cen-
   turies. In return for French help against the Austrians and the
   sanction of a single Italian state, Sardinia agreed in July 1858 at
   Plombières to cede to France the Alpine duchy of Savoy and the
   Mediterranean port of Nice.

4. Paul M. Ponziglione, S.J., to the Reverend Leopold Bushart, S.J.,
   Osage Mission, Kans., 20 May, 1884, St. Louis Province of the
   Society of Jesus Archives (hereafter cited as SLA).

5. James H. Defouri, V.G., "Rt. Rev. J.B. Miege, S.J., D.D," unpub-
   lished manuscript, n.d., copy in SLA.

6. Ibid., 1.

7. Garin, *Notices Biographiques,* 13–14.

8. Garin, *Les Évêques,* 46.

9. A. Usannaz to Bushart, New Orleans, 1 May 1884, SLA.

10. Garin, *Notices Biographiques,* 6–9.

11. Defouri, "Miege," 2.

12. Ibid., 3.

13. *Woodstock Letters* 13 (1884): 395, and Defouri, "Miege," 4. The former source seems to rely heavily on Defouri for this description.

Chapter 2: The Young Jesuit

1. Garin, *Notices Biographiques,* 14.

2. *Woodstock Letters* 13 (1884): 295.

3. Usannaz to Bushart, New Orleans, 1 May 1884, SLA.

4. Garin, *Notices Biographiques,* 15–17.

5. *Woodstock Letters* 15 (1884): 396.

6. Garin, *Notices Biographiques,* 15.

7. Ibid., 16–17.

8. Thomas Campbell, *The Jesuits 1534–1921*, vol. 2 (New York: Encyclopedia Press, 1821), 887–88. See also *Woodstock Letters* 13 (1884): 396.

9. Catalogs are located in the Missouri Province Archives, St. Louis, Mo. The catalogs from 1840 to 1854 are bound together. See "J.B. Miege" listing.

10. L. Curioz, S.J., to Usannaz, Spring Hill, Ala., 23 April 1884, file 3, SLA.

11. Garin, *Notices Biographiques,* 18.

12. Ibid., 19.

13. In his shorter manuscript biography of Miege, Defouri says he does not remember the date. He says only "he was ordained by a cardinal in his private chapel." However, in a letter to Ponziglione, Miege specifically mentions Cardinal Canali by name, 3 May 1884, SLA.

14. Garin, *Notices Biographiques,* 21–22.

15. Ibid., 23–24.

16. Curioz to Usannaz, Spring Hill, Ala., 23 April 1884, file 6, SLA.

17. Garin, *Notices Biographiques,* 26. One wonders who these *"terribles voraces si redoutes a ce moment"* (terrible, voracious creatures so feared at the time) were?

Chapter 3: To the American Missions

1. "Autobiography of Father Burchard Villiger, S.J.," *Woodstock Letters* 32 (1903): 65–66.

2. Defouri, "Miege," 5.

3. *Woodstock Letters* 30 (1901): 52.

4. John Baptist Miege to Urban Miege, St. Louis, Mo., in Garin, *Notices Biographiques,* 34. The letter was begun on 19 March 1849, but he did not finish it until the following September.

5. Garin, *Les Évêques,* 49; *Notices Biographiques,* 34.

6. Garin, *Notices Biographiques,* 35.

7. Ibid., 36–37.

8. Ibid., 37–38.

9. Ibid., 38–39. The cascade that Father Meige called Saint Antoine was most likely the present-day Coon Rapids as they appeared 150 years ago.

10. Ibid., 40.

11. Ibid., 41.

12. Ibid., 42.

13. Ibid., 43.

14. *Catalogi S.J. Missouri 1824–1868* (1849): 14 and (1850): 10. See also Garin, *Notices Biographiques,* 44.

15. John Baptist is thinking of the effect of such a statement on his brother. For a staunch clergyman, let alone a Jesuit, to be a republican (i.e., liberal) in the French or Italian sense would have been unthinkable at the time.

16. Ponziglione to Bushart, Osage Mission, Kans., 7 May 1884, SLA.

17. Garin, *Notices Biographiques,* 47.

18. John Elet to John Roothaan, St. Louis, Mo., 13 June 1849, in Gilbert J. Garraghan, S.J., *The Jesuits of the Middle United States,* vol. 2 (Chicago: Loyola University Press, 1984), 635–36.

19. Garraghan, *The Jesuits,* vol. 2, 636.

20. *Woodstock Letters* 13 (1884): 397; Defouri, "Miege," 6.

21. J. B. Miege to Samuel Eccleston, St. Louis, Mo., 17 October 1850, transcript in SLA.

22. Garraghan, *The Jesuits,* vol. 2, 638–39.

23. J. B. Miege to Urban, St. Louis, Mo., 1 November 1850, in Garin, *Notices Biographiques,* 47–48.

24. Garraghan, *The Jesuits,* vol. 2, 639.

25. Roothaan to J. B. Miege, [Rome?], 14 December 1850, in Garraghan, *The Jesuits,* vol. 2, 639. James A. McGonigle, writing in the *Leavenworth Times,* 1 June 1905, mentions that at the time there were only three bishops in the world who held their positions and still maintained membership in their respective orders.

26. Maurice Gailland, S.J., to J. B. Miege, Saint Mary's, Kans., 1 December 1850, SLA, copy University of Detroit Archives (hereafter cited as UDA).

27. J. B. Miege to Urban, St. Louis, Mo., 26 February 1851, in Garin, *Notices Biographiques,* 49–50.

28. J. B. Miege to Urban, St. Louis, Mo., 24 March 1851, in Garin, *Notices Biographiques,* 51.

29. *Leavenworth Daily Times,* 20 December 1874, letter to the editor from Thomas Ambrose Butler. There was a Reverend Ambrose Butler stationed as a chaplain at Fort Leavenworth at the time. They were probably one and the same.

Chapter 4: The Bishop Enters His Vicariate

1. J. B. Miege to Urban, St. Louis, Mo., 26 February 1851, in Garin, *Notices Biographiques,* 50. See also *Catalogus Provinciae Missourianae Societatis Jesu,* St. Louis, Mo. (1850): 14–16.

2. *Woodstock Letters* 30 (1901): 52–53.

3. J. B. Miege to Urban, St. Louis, Mo., 26 February 1851, in Garin, *Notices Biographiques,* 50.

4. *Woodstock Letters* 30 (1884): 52.

5. *Woodstock Letters* 13 (1884): 398.

6. Ponziglione to Bushart, Osage Mission, Kans., 7 May 1884, SLA.

7. Ibid., 2.

8. Garin, *Notices Biographiques,* 59.

9. Ibid., 3. In his letter to Father Walter Hill, Gailland says the date of arrival was 24 May (see *Woodstock Letters* 6 [1887]: 11). In a

letter dated 13 November 1851, he has 31 May. Compare Garragan, *The Jesuits,* vol. 2, 644, note.

10. For a detailed account of Indian claims and treaties of cession, see Garraghan, *The Jesuits,* vol. 2, 181–235 and John Gilmary Shea, *Catholic Missions among the Indian Tribes of the United States* (New York: E. Dunigan and Brother, 1855).

11. Bea Brady, *Religious Life of Fort Leavenworth 1890–1910* (Leavenworth, Kans.: Privately published, 1940), 4.

12. Shea, *Catholic Missions,* 465. When Miege says the Osage Mission was two hundred miles from Saint Mary's, as he once did, he is referring to the circuitous route that had to be taken at the time. There were no roads as such.

13. Ibid.

14. *Woodstock Letters* 6 (1877): 11–12.

15. Garin, *Notices Biographiques,* 60–61.

16. Ibid., 63.

17. Ponziglione to Bushart, Osage Mission, Kans., 7 May 1884, SLA.

18. Ibid., 5.

19. Garin, *Notices Biographiques,* 65.

20. Ibid., 67.

21. Ibid., 79.

22. *Litterae Annuae Missionis St. Francic de Hieronymo apud Osagios,* 1869, SLA.

23. *Litterae Annuae (Annual Letters),* 1854–62. Not signed but seems to have been written in Ponziglione's handwriting, SLA.

24. Reuben G. Thwaites, ed., *The Jesuit Relations and Allied Documents,* vol. 68 (New York: Pageant Book Co.), 267.

25. Garin, *Notices Biographiques,* 46.

26. *Historia Domus Missionis Osagianae (History of the Osage Mission),* 1869, SLA.

27. *Litterae Annuae (Annual Letters),* 1869–79, SLA.

28. J. B. Miege to Luke Lea, commissioner, Indian Office, Department of the Interior, Osage Mission, Kans., 18 July 1851. The film copy in the Federal Archives in Kansas City, Mo., notes that the letter was "copied and presented." Copy in UDA.

29. J. B. Miege to unidentified party, Leavenworth, Kans., 20 January 1862, copy in UDA.

30. M. Whitcomb Hess, "Bishop Miege, S.J.: A Page of American History," *Contemporary Review* 210 (January 1967): 37.

31. Garin, *Notices Biographiques,* 76.

32. S. W. Brewster, "Rev. Paul M. Ponziglione," *Kansas State Historical Society Collections* 11 (1905–06): 21.

33. J. B. Miege to Roothaan, (location unknown), 17 August 1852, Loyola University (Chicago) Archives, file 560 (hereafter cited as LUA).

34. Ibid.

35. J. B. Miege to Roothan, (location unknown), 9 July 1852, file 559, LUA.

36. For extensive coverage of the mission's finances compare Garraghan, *The Jesuits,* vol. 2, 648–54.

37. Ibid., 653–54.

38. Ibid., 655.

Chapter 5: The European Interlude

1. Roothaan to William Murphy, Rome, 30 October 1851, in Augustine C. Wand, S.J., "Pioneer Bishop of the Prairies," *The Benedictine Review* (summer 1949): 7.

2. J. B. Miege to Roothaan, Saint Mary's, Kans., 9 July 1852, manuscripts 5–XI 13, file 559, LUA.

3. J. B. Miege to Roothaan, Saint Mary's, Kans., 13 March 1853, manuscripts 5–XI, file 562, LUA.

4. Both Garin, *Les Évêques,* 52, and Wand, "Pioneer Bishop," 7, simply say he sailed or departed in April. Sister Mary Paul sets the sailing date as 19 May 1853. We assume that the earlier date refers to departure from the mission or from St. Louis. See Sister Mary Paul Fitzgerald, *John Baptist Miege, S.J. 1815–1884 First Vicar Apostolic of the Indian Territory: A Study in Frontier History* (New York: United States Catholic Historical Society, 1934), 313.

5. Garin, *Les Évêques,* 53.

6. Garin, *Notices Biographiques,* 83.

7. Peter De Smet, S.J., "To the Editor of the *Précis Historique,* Brussels," *History of the Western Missions and Missionaries* (New York: P. J. Kenedy, 1859), 121–23.

8. Garin, *Les Évêques,* 53.

9. Garin, *Notices Biographiques,* 88.

10. De Smet, *History of the Western Missions,* 122–23.

11. Ibid., 123–25.

12. Ibid., 126–27.

13. Otto L. Bettman, *The Good Old Days—They Were Terrible* (New York: Random House, 1974), 171, quoting George T. Strong.

14. De Smet, *History of the Western Missions,* 128.

15. Bettman, *The Good Old Days,* 180–81.

Chapter 6: The Coming of the White Settlers

1. J.B. Miege to the Vicar General, St. Louis, Mo., 15 April 1853, manuscripts 5–XI 17, file 564, LUA.

2. De Smet as in Garraghan, *The Jesuits,* vol. 3, 3.

3. Garraghan, *The Jesuits,* vol. 3, 2.

4. J.B. Miege to Urban, Saint Mary's, Kans., 28 December 1854, in Garin, *Notices Biographiques,* 102.

5. H. Story, *History of the Lincoln Diocese* (Lincoln, Neb.: n.p., n.d.), 31.

6. J.B. Miege to R. A. Shaffel, S.J., Detroit, Mich., 16 December 1878. [Location of archives unknown].

7. Story, *History of the Lincoln Diocese,* 31.

8. J. B. Miege to Shaffel, Detroit, Mich., 16 December 1878.

9. J. B. Miege to Father General Peter Beckx, Saint Mary's, Kans., 4 July 1855, copy in LUA.

10. Story, *History of the Lincoln Diocese,* 31.

11. *Woodstock Letters* 4 (1875): 67.

12. *Woodstock Letters* 1 (1872): 112, 121.

Chapter 7: The Move to Leavenworth

1. William J. McEvoy, *The "Old Cathedral" Parish 1855–1877* (Leavenworth, Kans.: Privately published for the Church of the Immaculate Conception, 1976?), 17.

2. J. B. Miege to Urban, Saint Mary's, Kans., 28 December 1854, in Garin, *Notices Biographiques,* 103.

3. McEvoy, *The "Old Cathedral" Parish,* 19.

4. Ibid., 17. H. Miles Moore, in *Early History of Leavenworth City and County* (Leavenworth, Kans.: Samuel Dodsworth Book Co., 1906), 157, states that "the first Catholic Church was built on the southwest corner of Kickapoo and Fifth streets in the fall of 1855, where the Parochial house now stands, by that grand old man, true and earnest, father of the church, as well as public spirited citizen and devoted Christian gentleman, whom to know was to love and admire, the Right Reverend Bishop Miege."

5. Ibid., 18.

6. Garin, *Notices Biographiques,* 106.

7. Ibid., 111.

8. According to a sermon by the Very Reverend William Boland, 24 April 1950, in St. Peter's Cathedral, Kansas City, Kans.

9. McEvoy, *The "Old Cathedral" Parish,* 18.

10. For a detailed account of the coming of the Benedictines to Kansas, see Peter Beckman, O.S.B., *Kansas Monks* (Atchison, Kans.: Benedictine College Press, 1957), 21–22.

11. Father Henry Lemke to Archabbot Boniface Wimmer, Doniphan, Kans., 28 August 1856, in Beckman, *Kansas Monks,* 21–22.

12. Beckman, *Kansas Monks,* 26.

13. Ibid., 42–43.

14. Peter Beckman, O.S.B., *The Catholic Church on the Kansas Frontier 1850–1877* (diss., Catholic University of America, 1943), 70–71.

15. J. B. Miege to Urban, Leavenworth, Kans., 18 December 1856, in Garin, *Notices Biographiques,* 115.

16. McEvoy, *The "Old Cathedral" Parish,* 19–20, and Fitzgerald, *John Baptist Miege, S.J.,* 328.

17. Ibid., *The "Old Cathedral" Parish,* 21.

18. *Westport Weekly Border Star,* as in Beckman, *The Catholic Church on the Kansas Frontier,* 55–56.

19. McEvoy, *The "Old Cathedral" Parish,* 21.

20. Sister Julia Gilmore, S.C.L., *We Came North* (St. Meinrad, Ind.: St. Meinrad Press, 1961, 13–14). See also J. H. Johnston, III, *They Came This Way* (Leavenworth, Kans.: Privately published, 1988), 41.

21. See Johnston, *They Came This Way,* 42, and Gilmore, *We Came North,* 14–15.

22. Blaine Burkey, O.F.M. Cap., "Friend of the Potawatomi May Soon Be Canonized," manuscript copy in UDA. See also Beverly Boyd, *Saint Philippine Duchesne 1769–1852: An Exhibit of Materials Drawn from the Holdings of the Kansas Collection* (Atchison, Kans.: Benedictine College Press, n.d.). Mother Duchesne was canonized on 3 July 1988.

23. John Gilmary Shea, *The Catholic Church in the United States,* vol. 4 (New York: E. Dunigan and Brother, 1892), 659.

24. Henry Shindler, *Fort Leavenworth: Its Churches and Schools 1827–1912* (n.p.: Army Services Schools Press, 1912), 91.

25. Ibid., 92.

26. See Brady, *Religious Life of Fort Leavenworth,* 7–8, and Shindler, *Fort Leavenworth,* 92–93.

Chapter 8: The Bishop Visits Pike's Peak

1. Larry R. Hafen, *Colorado Gold Rush Contemporary Letters and Reports 1858–1859* (Glendale, Calif.: Arthur H. Clark Co., 1941).

2. Writers' Program of the Works Projects Administration in the State of Colorado, American Guide Series, *Colorado* (New York: Hastings House, 1941), 55.

3. J. B. Miege to Urban, Leavenworth, Kans., 24 February 1859, in Garin, *Notices Biographiques,* 122–23.

4. J. B. Miege to Urban, Leavenworth, Kans., 15 July 1860, in Garin, *Notices Biographiques,* 123.

5. Ibid.

6. James H. Defouri, *Historical Sketch of the Catholic Church in New Mexico* (San Francisco: McCormick Bros., 1887), 47, as in Garraghan, *The Jesuits,* vol. 3, 15–16, note 23a.

7. J. B. Miege to Abbé Marjolet, Saint Mary's, Kans., 1 November 1852, in Garin, *Notices Biographiques,* 69–72.

8. Ibid.

9. Thomas F. O'Connor, ed., "An Early Episcopal Visitation of Colorado: 1860: Letters of the Rt. Rev. John Baptist Miege, S.J." Annotated by the Reverend William J. Howlett. *Mid-America,* vol. 7, no. 18 (1936): 269.

10. J.B. Miege to Urban, Leavenworth, Kans., 15 July 1860, in Garin, *Notices Biographiques,* 125–26.

11. Ibid., 126.

12. O'Connor, "An Early Episcopal Visitation," 271.

13. J. B. Miege to Urban, 6 June 1860, in Garin, *Notices Biographiques,* 126–27.

14. Ibid.

15. Mark Twain, *Roughing It* (Hartford, Conn.: American Publishing Co., 1888), 38.

16. William F. Zornow, *Kansas* (Norman, Okla.: University of Oklahoma Press, 1957), 65. See also Mae Lacy Baggs, *Colorado* (Boston: Page Co., 1918), 91.

17. W. J. Howlett, *Life of the Right Reverend Joseph P. Machebeuf* (Pueblo, Colo.: Franklin Press, 1908), 285, as in Beckman, *Catholic Church,* 59.

18. J. B. Miege to Urban, Leavenworth, Kans., 15 July 1860, in Garin, *Notices Biographiques,* 128.

Chapter 9: "Bleeding Kansas"

1. J. B. Miege to Urban, Leavenworth, Kans., 26 February 1856, in Garin, *Notices Biographiques,* 113.

2. J. B. Miege to Urban, Saint Mary's Kans., 28 December 1854, in Garin, *Notices Biographiques,* 103.

3. J. B. Miege to Father General Peter Beckx, Leavenworth, Kans., 12 January 1857, copy in LUA.

4. J. B. Miege to Urban, Saint Mary's, Kans., 1855, in Garin, *Notices Biographiques,* 105.

5. The Know Nothing Party was secret, as were the various nativist groups from which it sprang. When members of the party were

interrogated, they would answer that they knew nothing about it; hence the name.

6. Beckman, *Catholic Church,* 43.

7. Editorial quoted by Dr. George Anderson in a centennial lecture to faculty and students of Saint Benedict's College, Atchison, Kans., 26 January 1961.

8. Zornow, *Kansas,* 73.

9. Walter E. Connelly, *Quantrill and the Border Wars* (New York: Pageant Books, 1956), 346.

10. Connelly, *Quantrill,* 264–85.

11. Ponziglione to Bushart, Osage Mission, Kans., 7 May 1884, SLA.

12. *Lawrence State Journal* published an abbreviated edition on 1 October 1863. An editorial reported that 160 men and boys had been "butchered" and 180 buildings burned.

13. J. B. Mlege to Urban, Leavenworth, Kans., 25 July 1862, in Garin, *Notices Biographiques,* 132.

14. Sterling Price was governor of Missouri from 1853 to 1857. In 1861, he became major general of the state militia and, by March of the following year, major general of the entire Confederate forces. In 1864, he invaded Missouri, advancing as far as St. Louis and Jefferson City. He never reached Leavenworth, Kansas, however.

15. Ponziglione to Bushart, Osage Mission, Kans., 7 May 1889, SLA.

16. Francis X. De Coen to Johnston, Leavenworth, Kans., 8 October 1861, in Beckman, *Catholic Church,* 62–63.

17. *Catholic Telegraph,* 8 October 1862, as in Beckman, *Catholic Church,* 65.

18. Beckman, *Catholic Church,* 63–64.

19. Reverend Anton Kuhls, *A Few Reminiscences of Forty Years in Wyandotte County Kansas* (Kansas City, Kans.: Privately published, 1904), 28.

20. Ibid., 27.

21. American Protective Association was a secret anti-Catholic organization founded in 1887 in Clinton, Iowa. Similar to the Know Nothing Party, it relied on political activity to fight against the "danger" of Catholicism in the U.S.

22. Ponziglione to editors, Osage Mission, Kans., 31 December 1872, *Woodstock Letters* 2 (1873): 156.

23. Beckman, *Catholic Church,* 105.

24. J. B. Miege to Urban, Leavenworth, Kans. 14 January 1867, in Garin, *Notices Biographiques,* 140.

25. C. D. Clark and R. L. Roberts, *People of Kansas* (Topeka, Kans.: Kansas State Planning Board, 1936), 34ff, and in Beckman, *Catholic Church,* 77.

26. Beckman, *Catholic Church,* 101.

27. Ibid.

28. Ibid.

29. Father Paul Ponziglione's *Journal,* 2, as in Beckman, *Catholic Church,* 113–14.

30. Ponziglione to Thomas O'Neil, Osage Mission, Kans., December 1871, July 1872, December 1873, *Woodstock Letters* 1 (1872): 111–21, 2 (1873): 146–56, 3 (1874): 126–30.

31. Ibid.

Chapter 10: Building a Cathedral

1. Kuhls, *Reminiscences,* 30–31.

2. Ibid.

3. J. Neale Carman, "The Unwilling Bishop," *The Kansas Magazine* 20 (1952): 22.

4. J. B. Miege to Urban, Leavenworth, Kans., 21 January 1863, in Garin, *Notices Biographiques,* 134.

5. Roothaan to J. B. Miege, Rome, 30 November 1850, as in Garraghan, *The Jesuits,* vol. 2, 639.

6. James F. Meline, *Two Thousand Miles on Horseback, Santa Fe and Back: A Summer Tour Through Kansas, Nebraska, Colorado, and New Mexico in the Year 1866* (New York: Hurd and Houghton, 1867), 2, as in Garraghan, *The Jesuits,* vol. 3, 21.

7. J. B. Miege to Urban, Leavenworth, Kans., 14 January 1867, in Garin, *Notices Biographiques,* 140.

8. J. B. Miege to Urban, Leavenworth, Kans., 15 November 1860, in Garin, *Notices Biographiques,* 130–31.

9. Beckman, *Catholic Church,* 75.

10. J. B. Miege to Urban, Leavenworth, Kans., 26 July 1864, in Garin, *Notices Biographiques,* 135–36.

11. Ibid.

12. See *The Conservative,* 20 September 1861; *Leavenworth Daily Times,* 20 September 1864, in McEvoy, *The "Old Cathedral" Parish,* 24–25.

13. *Daily Times* and *Conservative,* 9 December 1858.

14. Garraghan, *The Jesuits,* vol. 3, 20–21. See also McEvoy, *The "Old Cathedral" Parish,* 28.

15. James Andrew McGonigle, *Kansas Historical Collection* 9 (1905–06): 159, as in Garraghan, *The Jesuits,* vol. 3, 21.

16. Garin, *Notices Biographiques,* 139.

17. J. B. Miege to M. J. Spalding, Leavenworth, Kans., 26 August 1866, typed copy of letter and letter of resignation in UDA.

18. J. B. Miege to Urban, Leavenworth, Kans., 14 January 1867, in Garin, *Notices Biographiques,* 139–40.

19. J. B. Miege to Urban, Leavenworth, Kans., 15 August 1868, in Garin, *Notices Biographiques,* 142.

20. McEvoy, *The "Old Cathedral" Parish,* 26–27.

21. *Leavenworth Daily Times,* 9 December 1868.

22. Ibid. The cathedral seated about 1,100. For the occasion additional seats were likely brought in.

23. Oscar Ericson, c. 1928, copy in SLA.

24. McEvoy, *The "Old Cathedral" Parish,* 52–53.

Chapter 11: Bishop Miege and Vatican Council I

1. J. B. Miege to Urban, Leavenworth, Kans., 14 January 1867, in Garin, *Notices Biographiques,* 142.

2. Garin, *Notices Biographiques,* 143.

3. J. B. Miege to Propaganda, copy of the document, originally in Latin, n.p., n.d., SLA. Translation appears in Garraghan, *The Jesuits,* vol. 3, 19–20.

4. Address of Father Himos to Bishop Miege, *Leavenworth*

Commercial, 18 September 1869, reprinted in *The Western Watchman,* 10 April 1869.

5. Garin, *Notices Biographiques,* 144–45.

6. Ibid., 145–46.

7. Thomas P. Neill and Raymond H. Schmandt, *History of the Catholic Church* (Milwaukee, Wis.: Bruce, 1957), 530–35. For an excellent and more detailed account of the Council, compare Cuthbert Butler, *The Vatican Council,* 2 vols. (London: Longmans, Green, 1930).

8. J. B. Miege to Canon Alliaudi, Leavenworth, Kans., 30 January 1870, in Garin, *Notices Biographiques,* 148.

9. Neill and Schmandt, *History of the Catholic Church,* 532.

10. Ibid.

11. J. B. Miege to Canon Alliaudi, Leavenworth, Kans., 30 January 1870, in Garin, *Notices Biographiques,* 148.

12. Cf. James J. Hennesey, S.J., *The First Council of the Vatican: The American Experience* (New York: Herder and Herder, 1963), especially chap. 3, "Preliminaries to the Debate on Infallibility." Hennesey offers a scholarly account of the American hierarchy's attitude on the doctrine.

13. Butler, *Vatican Council,* vol. 1, 27.

14. Butler includes a brief but excellent account of Gallicanism in *Vatican Council,* vol. 1, 23–24.

15. Although Auguste Joseph Alphonse Gratry, the French theologian and professor of moral theology at the Sorbonne, vehemently opposed the dogma of papal infallibility, he accepted the decrees when finally enacted.

16. J. B. Miege to Alliaudi, Leavenworth, Kans., 30 January 1870, in Garin, *Notices Biographiques,* 147.

17. J. B. Miege to Alliaudi, (location unknown), 20 April 1870, in Garin, *Notices Biographiques,* 150.

18. Neill and Schmandt, *History of the Catholic Church,* 533. Dollinger's supporters formed a schismatic group known as the Old Catholics.

19. Neill and Schmandt, *History of the Catholic Church,* 533–34.

20. Joseph McSorley, *An Outline History of the Church by Centuries,* 6th rev. ed. (St. Louis, Mo.: B. Herder, 1947), 814–16. See also Butler, *The Vatican Council,* vol. 2, 166.

21. Garin, *Notices Biographiques,* 151.

22. *Leavenworth Daily Times,* 22 November 1870. See also (Leavenworth) *Monitor,* translated in its entirety by *l'Echo des Alpes,* 8 and 15 January 1871, and cited in Garin, *Notices Biographiques,* 152–62.

Chapter 12: The South American Experience

1. McEvoy, *The "Old Cathedral" Parish,* 30. See also Garin, *Notices Biographiques,* 203.

2. J. B. Miege to Urban, Leavenworth, Kans., 10 September 1871, in Garin, *Notices Biographiques,* 168.

3. Beckx to J. B. Miege, Rome, 23 July 1871, copy of the original Latin and transcript in UDA. See also Garraghan, *The Jesuits,* vol. 3, 23.

4. Beckx to J. B. Miege, Rome, 2 November 1871, copy of the original Latin in UDA.

5. Garin, *Notices Biographques,* 168.

6. Beckman, *Kansas Monks,* 90.

7. Garin, *Notices Biographiques,* 166.

8. Ibid.

9. J. B. Miege to Urban, San Francisco, 23 October 1871, in Garin, *Notices Biographiques,* 170–71. The colleges referred to are the present Jesuit-run University of San Francisco and Santa Clara University.

10. Ibid., 171.

11. J. B. Miege to Urban, Santiago, Chile, 4 November 1872, in Garin, *Notices Biographiques,* 172–73.

12. Ibid.

13. Ibid., 174–75.

14. J. B. Miege to Theodore Heimann, Cordova, Argentine Republic, 20 April 1873. Letter quoted in McEvoy, *The "Old Cathedral" Parish,* 32.

15. Garin, *Notices Biographiques,* 176.

16. Ibid.

17. J. B. Miege to Urban, Cordova, Argentine Republic, 8 April 1873, in Garin, *Notices Biographiques,* 177.

18. Ibid., 178. The route used by the bishop's party was likely over the Uspiata Pass.

19. Ibid. Since Jason was a wool merchant, his wife would have had no silk garments. Hence, what remained of the traveler was nothing.

20. Ibid., 179.

21. Garin, *Notices Biographiques,* 179–80.

22. Ibid., 181.

23. Ibid.

24. Ibid., 183.

25. Ibid., 183–84.

26. Ibid., 184.

27. Ibid., 185. The Jesuits began their work in Paraguay in 1587, coming east of the Andes on the invitation of the bishops of Tucumán and Asunción. The colleges established by the Jesuits, particularly that in Cordova, which attained the rank of university in 1622, were in time to become the seats of learning in the area. See L. Schmidt, ed., *Synopsis historiae Societatis Jesu* (Ratisbonae, Bavaria [now Regensburg, Germany]: Frederic Pustet, 1914), 345.

Chapter 13: Brazil and the Voyage North

1. J. B. Miege to Urban, Rio de Janeiro, 3 March 1873, in Garin, *Notices Biographiques,* 185.

2. Ibid., 186.

3. Ibid., 186–87.

4. Ibid., 187.

5. Ibid., 187–88.

6. J. B. Miege to Urban, Itu, Brazil, 15 January 1847, in Garin, *Notices Biographiques,* 190–91.

7. The Marquis de Pombal, as Minister of State, was chiefly responsible for the Jesuits' expulsion in 1759 from Portugal and its colonies; hence, also from Brazil. Ironically, when Pombal died—and after falling out of favor in Portugal—the Jesuits gave him an honorable burial. Later, several of his grandsons entered the Society.

8. *New Catholic Encyclopedia,* 6th ed., s.v. "Freemasonry."

9. J. B. Miege to Urban, Itu, Brazil, 15 January 1874, in Garin, *Notices Biographiques,* 191.

10. Ibid., 192.

11. J. B. Miege to Urban, Puerto Rico, 4 April 1874, in Garin, *Notices Biographiques,* 193. This persecution of the bishops backfired on the government. The people of Brazil were not about to see their bishops treated so badly. Church services began to be filled to capacity, and a real religious revival took place. In the end, victory belonged to the bishops.

12. J. B. Miege to Urban, Havana, Cuba, 19 April 1874, in Garin, *Notices Biographiques,* 194.

13. Ibid., 195.

14. J. B. Miege to Urban, Leavenworth, Kans., July 1874, in Garin, *Notices Biographiques,* 199.

15. J. B. Miege to Urban, Havana, Cuba, 19 April 1874, in Garin, *Notices Biographiques,* 196.

16. J. B. Miege to Urban, Leavenworth, Kans., July 1874, in Garin, *Notices Biographiques,* 199–200.

17. Ibid., 200–201.

Chapter 14: Bishop Miege Retires

1. *The Leavenworth Daily Times,* 27 May 1874.

2. J. B. Miege to Urban, Leavenworth, Kans., July 1874, in Garin, *Notices Biographiques,* 200.

3. Garraghan, *The Jesuits,* vol. 3, 23.

4. Garin, *Les Évêques,* 64.

5. Garin, *Notices Biographiques,* 200.

6. Ibid., 201.

7. J. B. Miege to Urban, Leavenworth, Kans., 24 November 1874, in Garin, *Notices Biographiques,* 202.

8. Ibid., 203–4.

9. Copy of original document in Latin, SLA, copy in UDA.

10. J. B. Miege to Joseph-Eugene Miege, Leavenworth, Kans., 15 December 1874, in Garin, *Notices Biographiques,* 206.

11. J. B. Miege to Alliaudi, St. Louis, Mo., 8 January 1875, in Garin, *Notices Biographiques,* 207.

12. J. B. Miege to Joseph-Eugene, St. Louis, Mo., 17 February 1875, in Garin, *Notices Biographiques,* 211–12.

13. J. B. Miege to Alliaudi, St. Louis, Mo., 8 January 1875, in Garin, *Notices Biographiques,* 208–9.

14. Copy in SLA, B M58, UDA.

15. Address written by clergy of Leavenworth diocese, 4 January 1875, SLA, copy in UDA.

16. *The Leavenworth Daily Times,* 15 December, 1874.

17. Thomas Ambrose Butler, letter to the editor, *Leavenworth Daily Times,* 20 December 1874. Father Butler was one of Bishop Miege's diocesan clergy as well as a staunch supporter of the bishop.

18. Kuhls, *Reminiscences,* 36.

19. *History of the Sisters of Charity of Leavenworth,* (Kansas City: n.p., 1898), 153–54, as in Fitzgerald, *John Baptist Miege,* 351.

20. J. B. Miege to Alliaudi, St. Louis, Mo., 8 January 1875, in Garin, *Notices Biographiques,* 210.

21. J. B. Miege to Joseph-Eugene, St. Louis, Mo., 17 February 1875, in Garin, *Notices Biographiques,* 211–12.

22. J. B. Miege to Joseph-Eugene, Woodstock, Md., 11 December 1875, in Garin, *Notices Biographiques,* 214.

23. Ibid.

24. J. B. Miege to Alliaudi, Woodstock, Md., 24 May 1876, in Garin, *Notices Biographiques,* 216.

25. Ibid., 217.

Chapter 15: The Detroit College President

1. George Paré, *Catholic Church in Detroit* (Detroit: Gabriel Richard Press, 1951), 548.

2. Beckx to O'Neil, Fiesole, Italy, 16 February 1877, Missouri Province Archives (hereafter cited as MPA).

3. Beckx to O'Neil, Rome, 21 April 1877, MPA.

4. Document giving the Society of Jesus the cathedral church of SS. Peter and Paul with surrounding property in return for establishing a college in Detroit, 5 April 1877, copy in UDA.

5. Detroit College Diary, 1 and 2 June 1877, UDA.

6. "The Society of Jesus," *The Evening News* (Detroit), 8 June 1877.

7. Diary, 16 June 1877, UDA.

8. Ibid.

9. *Evening News,* 17 July 1877.

10. "Detroit College," *Detroit Free Press,* 12 July 1877. See also *Detroit College Catalogue,* 1877.

11. The program leading to a bachelor's degree took seven years to complete and was divided into two departments: collegiate, comparable to our modern college, and academic, comparable to our modern high school. The collegiate program took place during the final four years: philosophy, rhetoric, poetry, and humanities corresponded to our senior, junior, sophomore, and freshman classes. The program in Detroit started with second and third academic. Then a more advanced class would be added each year until the program was complete.

12. J. B. Miege to Alliaudi, Detroit, Mich., 1878, in Garin, *Notices Biographiques,* 219. Although Garin attaches no specific date to the letter, it was probably written in late summer 1878.

13. J. B. Miege to Alliaudi, Detroit, Mich., in Garin, *Notices Biographiques,* 220. The letter was probably written in early 1879.

14. Diary, 21 February 1878. Newspaper clipping is not dated. For a fuller account of the "happenings" during Father Miege's presidency at Detroit College, see Herman Muller, *The University of Detroit 1877–1977* (Detroit, Mich.: University of Detroit Press, 1976).

15. Garin, *Notices Biographiques,* 223.

Chapter 16: The Last Years

1. J. B. Miege to Joseph-Eugene, Woodstock, Md., 29 September 1880, in Garin, *Notices Biographiques,* 223–24. In effect, he was the "spiritual father" or counselor of the students at Woodstock College.

2. J. B. Miege to Alliaudi, Woodstock, Md., 1 December 1880, in Garin, *Notices Biographiques,* 225–26. James A. Garfield, a Republican, was elected president in the November 1880 elections.

3. Ibid., 226.

4. Ibid., 226–27.

5. J. B. Miege, Last Will and Testament, 4 March 1881, copy in UDA.

6. J. B. Miege to Alliaudi, Woodstock, Md., 10 January 1882, in Garin, *Notices Biographiques,* 227–28.

7. J. B. Miege to Alliaudi, Woodstock, Md., 1 November 1882, in Garin, *Notices Biographiques,* 229.

8. The 1990 census figures gives the total U. S. population as 250,870,030; the Roman Catholic population as 55,646,713.

9. J. B. Miege to Alliaudi, Woodstock, Md., 1 November 1882, in Garin, *Notices Biographiques,* 229–30.

10. Ibid., 230. Miege is not too clear. What did he mean by "Germans" in 1853? Was he equating Anglo-Saxon Americans with Germans? I would tend to think so.

11. Ibid., 231.

12. J. B. Miege to Alliaudi, Woodstock, Md., 18 December 1882, in Garin, *Notices Biographiques,* 232.

13. J. B. Miege to Marjolet, Woodstock, Md., 4 March 1883, in Garin, *Notices Biographiques,* 232–33.

14. J. B. Miege to Alliaudi, Woodstock, Md., 17 October 1883, in Garin, *Notices Biographiques,* 234–35.

15. Father Rector John Bapst to Sister Saint-Louis, Woodstock, Md., 14 December 1883, in Garin, *Notices Biographiques,* 235.

16. Bapst to Sister Saint-Louis, Woodstock, Md., 3 August 1884, in Garin, *Notices Biographiques,* 236.

17. Very Reverend James Defouri, V. G., Santa Fe, N.M., late 1884, seven handwritten pages, composed after hearing of J.B. Miege's death, copy in UDA.

18. Ponziglione to Bushart, Osage Mission, Kans., 7 May 1884, eight-page document, SLA.

19. "Father John B. Miege," *Woodstock Letters* 13 (1884): 394–97.

20. Sermon by the Very Reverend William T. J. Boland, 24 April 1950, printed copy in UDA.

BIBLIOGRAPHY

Unpublished Manuscript Sources

Beckx, Peter to J. B. Miege. 2 November 1871. University of Detroit Archives, Detroit, Mich.

Beckx, Peter to Thomas O'Neil. 16 February 1877. Missouri Province Archives, St. Louis, Mo.

Beckx, Peter to Thomas O'Neil. 21 April 1877. Missouri Province Archives, St. Louis, Mo.

Boland, Very Reverend William T. J. Sermon. 24 April 1950. University of Detroit Archives, Detroit, Mich.

Burkey, Blaine. "Friend of the Potawatomi May Soon Be Canonized." University of Detroit Archives, Detroit, Mich.

Catalogus Provinciae Missourianae Societatis Jesu. 1850. University of Detroit Jesuit Archives, Detroit, Mich.

Clergy of Leavenworth diocese. Testimonial honoring J. B. Miege. St. Louis Province of the Society of Jesus Archives, St. Louis, Mo.

Committee of Leavenworth Cathedral parishioners. Testimonial honoring J. B. Miege. 1874. St. Louis Province of the Society of Jesus Archives, St. Louis, Mo.

Curioz, L. to A. Usannaz. 23 April 1884. St. Louis Province of the Society of Jesus Archives, St. Louis, Mo.

Defouri, James A. "Rt. Rev. J. B. Miege, S.J., D.D." St. Louis Province of the Society of Jesus Archives, St. Louis, Mo.

———. Testimonial written after hearing of J. B. Miege's death. Late 1884. University of Detroit Archives, Detroit, Mich.

Detroit College Diary. University of Detroit Jesuit Archives, Detroit, Mich.

Gailland, Maurice to J. B. Miege. 1 December 1850. St. Louis Province of the Society of Jesus Archives, St. Louis, Mo.

Historia Domus Missionis Osagianae. 1869. St. Louis Province of the Society of Jesus Archives, St. Louis, Mo.

Litterae Annuae. 1854–62. St. Louis Province of the Society of Jesus Archives, St. Louis, Mo.

Litterae Annuae. 1869–79. St. Louis Province of the Society of Jesus Archives, St. Louis, Mo.

Litterae Annuae Missionis St. Francic de Hieronymo apud Osagios. 1869. St. Louis Province of the Society of Jesus Archives, St. Louis, Mo.

Miege, J.B. Last will and testament. 4 March 1881. University of Detroit Archives.

Miege, J. B. to Peter Beckx. 4 July 1855. Loyola University Archives, Chicago.

Miege, J. B. to Samuel Eccleston. 17 October 1850. St. Louis Province of the Society of Jesus Archives, St. Louis, Mo.

Miege, J. B. to Father General Peter Beckx. 12 January 1857. Loyola University Archives, Chicago.

Miege, J. B. to Luke Lea. 18 July 1851. University of Detroit Archives, Detroit, Mich.

Miege, J. B. to John Roothaan. 13 March 1853. Loyola University Archives, Chicago.

Miege, J. B. to John Roothaan. 9 July 1852. Loyola University Archives, Chicago.

Miege, J. B. to John Roothaan. 17 August 1852. Loyola University Archives, Chicago.

Miege, J. B. to R. A. Shaffel. 16 December 1878. [Location of archives unknown].

Miege, J. B. to M. J. Spalding. 26 August 1866. University of Detroit Archives, Detroit, Mich.

Miege, J. B. to unidentified party. 20 January 1862. University of Detroit Archives, Detroit, Mich.

Miege, J. B. to Vicar General. 15 April 1853. Loyola University Archives, Chicago.

Ponziglione, Paul M. to Leopold Bushart. 7 May 1884. St. Louis Province of the Society of Jesus Archives, St. Louis, Mo.

Ponziglione, Paul M. to Leopold Bushart. 20 May 1884. St. Louis Province of the Society of Jesus Archives, St. Louis, Mo.

Usannaz, A. to Leopold Bushart. 1 May 1884. St. Louis Province of the Society of Jesus Archives, St. Louis, Mo.

Printed Manuscript Sources

Garin, Joseph. *Les Évêques et Prêtres de Chevron.* Albertville, France: Librairie M. Papet, 1936.

————. *Notices Biographiques sur Mgr. J.-B. Miége Premier Vicaire Apostolique du Kansas.* Moûtiers, France: Imprimerie Cane Soeurs, 1886.

Thwaites, Reuben G. *The Jesuit Relations and Allied Documents.* 72 vols. New York: Pageant Book Co., 1959.

Woodstock Letters: A Record of Current Events and Historical Notes Connected with the Colleges and Missions of the Society of Jesus. 98 vols. Woodstock, Md., 1872–1969.

Newspapers

The Conservative (Leavenworth), 20 September 1861.

Detroit Free Press, 12 July 1877.

The Evening News (Detroit), 8 June 1877; 17 July 1877.

Leavenworth Times, 1 June 1905.

Leavenworth Daily Times, 1864–74.

Leavenworth Commercial, 18 September 1869.

l'Echo des Alpes, 8 and 15 January 1871.

The Western Watchman, 10 April 1869.

Periodicals

Brewster, S. W., "Rev. Paul M. Ponziglione." *Kansas State Historical Society Collections* 11 (1905–06).

Carman, J. Neale. "The Unwilling Bishop." *Kansas Magazine* (1952): 17–22.

———. "The Bishop East of the Rockies Views his Diocesans, 1851–1853." *The Kansas Historical Quarterly* 21 (summer 1954): 81–86.

Hess, M. Whitcomb. "Bishop Miege, S.J. A Page of American History." *Contemporary Review* (January 1967): 36–39.

O'Connor, Thomas F. "An Early Episcopal Visitation of Colorado; 1860: Letters of the Rt. Rev. John Baptist Miege, S.J." Annotated by the Reverend William J. Howlett. *Mid-America,* no. 18 (1936): 266–71.

Wand, Augustine C., S.J. "Pioneer Bishop of the Prairies." *The Benedictine Review* (summer 1949): 5–11, 46–50.

Books

Baggs, Mae Lacy. *Colorado.* Boston: Page Co., 1918.

Beckman, Peter, O.S.B. *The Catholic Church on the Kansas Frontier* 1850–1877. Diss. Catholic University of America, 1943.

———. *Kansas Monks.* Atchison, Kans.: Benedictine College Press, 1957.

Bettman, Otto L. *The Good Old Days—They Were Terrible.* New York: Random House, 1974.

Boyd, Beverly. *Saint Philippine Duchesne 1769–1852.* Atchison, Kans.: Benedictine College Press, 1987.

Brady, Bea. *Religious Life of Fort Leavenworth 1890–1910.* Leavenworth, Kans.: Privately published, 1940.

Butler, Cuthbert. *The Vatican Council.* 2 vols. London: Longmans, Green, 1930.

Campbell, Thomas. *The Jesuits 1534–1921.* 2 vols. New York: Encyclopedia Press, 1921.

Clark, C. D., and R. L. Roberts. *People of Kansas.* Topeka, Kans.: Kansas State Planning Board, 1936.

Connelly, Walter E. *Quantrill and the Border Wars.* New York: Pageant Book Co., 1956.

Defouri, James H. *Historical Sketch of the Catholic Church in New Mexico.* San Francisco: McCormick Bros., 1887.

De Smet, Peter, S.J. *History of the Western Missions and Missionaries.* New York: P.J. Kenedy, 1859.

Fitzgerald, Mary Paul. *John Baptist Miege, S.J. 1815–1884 First Vicar Apostolic of the Indian Territory: A Study in Frontier History.* New York: United States Catholic Historical Society, 1934.

Garraghan, Gilbert J., S.J. *The Jesuits of the Middle United States.* 3 vols. Chicago: Loyola University Press, 1984.

Gilmore, Sister Julia, S.C.L. *We Came North.* St. Meinrad, Ind.: St. Meinrad, 1961.

Hafen, Larry R. *Colorado Gold Rush Contemporary Letters and Reports 1858–1859.* Glendale, Calif.: Arthur H. Clark Co., 1941.

Hennesey, James J., S.J. *The First Council of the Vatican. The American Experience.* New York: Herder and Herder, 1963.

History of the Sisters of Charity of Leavenworth. Kansas City: n.p., 1898.

Howlett, W. J. *Life of the Right Reverend Joseph P. Machebeuf.* Pueblo, Colo.: Franklin Press, 1908.

Johnston, J. J., III. *They Came This Way.* Leavenworth, Kans.: Privately published, 1988.

Kuhls, Anton. *A Few Reminiscences of Forty Years in Wyandotte County Kansas*. Kansas City, Kans.: Privately published, 1904.

McEvoy, William J. *The "Old Cathedral" Parish 1855–1877*. Leavenworth, Kans.: Privately published for the Church of the Immaculate Conception, [1976?].

McSorley, Joseph. *An Outline History of the Church by Centuries*. 6th rev. ed. St. Louis, Mo.: B. Herder, 1947.

Meline, James F. *Two Thousand Miles on Horseback, Sante Fe and Back: A Summer Tour through Kansas, Nebraska, Colorado, and New Mexico in the Year 1866*. New York: Hurd and Houghton, 1867.

Moore, H. Miles. *Early History of Leavenworth City and County*. Leavenworth, Kans.: Samuel Dodsworth Book Co., 1906.

Muller, Herman, S.J. *The University of Detroit 1877–1977*. Detroit, Mich.: University of Detroit Press, 1976.

Neill, Thomas P., and Raymond H. Schmandt. *History of the Catholic Church*. Milwaukee, Wis.: Bruce, 1957.

Paré, George. *Catholic Church in Detroit*. Detroit, Mich.: Gabriel Richard Press, 1951.

Schmidt, L. ed. *Synopsis historiae Societatis Jesu*. Ratisbonae, Bavaria [now Regensburg, Germany]: Frederic Pustet, 1914.

Shea, John Gilmary. *Catholic Missions among the Indian Tribes of the United States*. New York: E. Dunigan and Brother, 1855.

————. *The Catholic Church in the United States*. 4 vols. New York: E. Dunigan and Brother, 1892.

Shindler, Henry. *Fort Leavenworth: Its Churches and Schools 1827–1912*. N.p.: Army Service Schools Press, 1912.

Story, H. *History of the Lincoln Diocese*. Lincoln, Neb.: N.p., n.d.

Twain, Mark. *Roughing It*. Hartford, Conn.: American Publishing Co., 1888.

Writers' Program of the Work Projects Administration in the State of Colorado. American Guide Series. *Colorado*. New York: Hastings House, 1941.

Zornow, William F. *Kansas*. Norman, Okla.: University of Oklahoma Press, 1957.

INDEX